Pooja Lamba Cheema is a 40-year-old mother of two. She hails from Delhi but has spent the last 15 years of her life in small towns across the country. She is a postgraduate in business management, but writing has always been her first love. Having a spiritual bent of mind led her to explore the practice of vipassanā meditation. Her stay at a vipassanā ashram had a powerful impact on her mind and life and led her to write this book: an amalgam of a memoir and a spiritual quest.

VIPASSANĀ
THE JOURNEY OF
A THOUSAND STEPS

Pooja Lamba Cheema

Hay House Publishers India

Australia • Canada • Hong Kong • India
South Africa • United Kingdom • United States

Hay House Publishers (India) Pvt. Ltd.
Muskaan Complex, Plot No.3, B-2 Vasant Kunj, New Delhi-110 070, India
Hay House Inc., PO Box 5100, Carlsbad, CA 92018-5100, USA
Hay House UK, Ltd., Astley House, 33 Notting Hill Gate, London W11 3JQ, UK
Hay House Australia Pty Ltd., 18/36 Ralph St., Alexandria NSW 2015, Australia
Hay House SA (Pty) Ltd., PO Box 990, Witkoppen 2068, South Africa
Hay House Publishing, Ltd., 17/F, One Hysan Ave., Causeway Bay, Hong Kong
Raincoast, 9050 Shaughnessy St., Vancouver, BC V6P 6E5, Canada

Email: contact@hayhouse.co.in
www.hayhouse.co.in

ISBN 978- 93-81398-77-7
ISBN 978-93-84544-30-0 (e-book)

Printed and bound at
Rajkamal Electric Press, Sonipat, Haryana (India)

This book is dedicated to my late parents,
Jasbir Singh and Veena Lamba,
and to my beloved children,
Sartaj and Afreen.

Contents

Acknowledgements

I WOULD LIKE TO THANK THE LATE SHRI S. N. GOENKA, who introduced so many of us to the wonderful path of Dhamma and the miracle of insight. Without his selfless effort towards setting up numerous meditation centres, which impart the knowledge of the ancient technique of vipassanā meditation taught by the Buddha, I would never have been able to assimilate the wonderment and purpose of human life and never known the meaning of real joy, real peace and real happiness.

I would also like to thank Dr Vineet Agarwal, without whom I would never have embarked on this amazing journey of spiritual liberation. A special thanks to Gary Dhillon, who believed in the book from the beginning and offered his unrelenting encouragement and support to see it published.

This book is also for the unwitting support group of my 'soul sisters,' Louisa, Anuradha, Snigdha and Priya, who traversed in silence the same journey that I did.

Lastly, I would like to thank Hay House Publishers for seeing beauty in my book.

PROLOGUE

YESTERDAY, I WAS APPREHENSIVE. TODAY, I AM OSCILLATING between apprehension and expectation. I feel cleansed as I take off my adornments. I trim my long nails. I feel only a brief twinge of remorse. I have often wanted to revert to a state of pristine naturalness and fantasized about cutting my hair short and wearing only a robe for the rest of my life. Adornments and accoutrements take up too much mind space and waste time. We lose ourselves under layers of appearance. Society conditions us that way. And that would make up two of the many lesser reasons why I am going away. I want the layers to be peeled away and I want to let go of many of the ideas and beliefs that are a result of my conditioning.

I have knots in my stomach. I am poised at a threshold. Never before have I gone to this extent to purge my being of emotional bonds. I have struggled and endeavoured, but never taken a plunge of this kind. I would not have been able to do this on my own. I thought I was too stoic and resilient to need all this; even if I often break with the overwhelming burden of pain. On the face of it, I still function as a normal being; a mother and a wife, fulfilling my obligations. Maybe it is because I have two opposing directions in my sun sign. So, even as I break down inside with the tumult of silent emotion, I also laugh and revel. That dichotomy is me:

the being of contradiction; the spiritualist, the realist, the aggressor, the pushover, the sinner and the saint.

But I do not want to be a leaf in the wind any longer; adrift and ready to be swept in any direction the winds chose to take me, even if it means the death of illusion and the fading away of the colours that have made up my life: the colours of autumn and spring, winter and even blazing summer, the colours of hope and of its death, the colours of joy tainted with sorrow and of sorrow mingled with hope, the bleak, dark colours of loss of faith and hope; the grey of betrayal and deceit, the black of mourning and grieving. And then the brighter colours: colours of love and rejoicing and temporary insanity, colours of birth and renewal, colours of rising from the ashes time and again like my favourite proverbial phoenix.

Kahlil Gibran wrote, 'Your pain is the breaking of the shell that encloses your understanding.' I feel the breaking of the shell brings understanding. I am going to be learning about the impermanence of things and to be able to feel like the calm centre in the middle of the hurricane that is life and be unlike the people around me, always on a mission to achieve, without realizing that most of what truly matters lies beyond the ambit of what they hope to attain. I hope to rejuvenate that part of me which is eroded and jaded. I hope to re-colour my life. The grey and the black will come: they are destiny's children. I must paint my world in the brightest colours, to see what life really has to offer me if I open up my soul to its blessings and its miracles.

I recently read a story called 'White feather' about a woman who wishes she could find a talisman in the form of a white feather, which would give her hope in a life full of struggle: near bankruptcy, being a single parent and the sole caregiver to her ailing parent. She starts obsessing about it, but knows it is a fantastical wish. However, on a particularly hard day, when she gets back home from work;

there it is – a white feather sitting on the front steps to her door. From that moment on, she feels her life is changed. The story made me yearn for my own talisman. I wish I could find a white feather before I left. Or maybe not. This is not about believing in miracles and signs: it is about strengthening one's mind to a point where one can observe without reacting. A white feather would take me back to a fairy tale. I must not think of white feathers. This is about reducing one's yearning; needless yearning of the life of fairy tales. Melancholy comes with yearning; they are twin sisters. I want to break my familiar ties with them. I want to find new family in determination, strife and positivity.

Such were my thoughts two days before I left. On the day I was supposed to leave, I was in a state of agitation. I thought about my refuge, two hours away. Twenty acres of refuge to heal, wander, think, meditate and generally lose myself in a trance, praying to God with the faint smell of incense hovering in the air and an image of *Om* in front of my closed eyes, as I went deep into *bhakti*.

Though many storms raged silently inside, I was a pillar of strength to a friend of mine who needed hope and a reason to go on living. When one's own heart is in the grip of emotion, one is unable to practically live one's philosophies. He hung on to each word like a drowning man to a lifeboat. I gave him all the strength I did not have. I was going away to become strong, but I knew he did not have the hope of any refuge in the near future.

Positive thoughts give temporary sanity and peace and a kind of resignation that pain is inevitable; that there is a quiet, necessary beauty to it; something that one needs, to evolve into a better, wiser being, like the breaking of a cocoon to release the butterfly within. That is what we grow up with: acceptance of pain, expectation of pain and slow, painful healing of pain.

I said goodbye to two friends who mattered. One was my

saviour; I could almost see him beaming as I spoke to him. I asked him by way of one last useless plea, what I would gain by running away from reality. His calm response was that I was not running away from reality. I would confront it as I had never confronted it before. The other tried to persuade me not to renounce the world for twelve days. He promised me an evening of revelry at the best restaurant if I dropped my plans. He was scared of the anguish which was causing me to go away. The advice of practical people is always to deal with every situation squarely and remain happy. It's good advice, but easier said than done. There really was no choice for me; no other refuge. I smiled sadly inside and joked with him that he was on for the evening. Then I said goodbye and switched off my phone.

As I write this at home on my first day back, I think I hear the sound of the little bells of the pagoda. They hung like bunches of grapes from the spires rising from the top of the structure. The tinkling sounded like a wind chime. The sound takes me back to those environs of serenity and hope.

In retrospect, I was heading for this experience. For many months prior to my going away, I had been unable to lose myself in senseless revelry or frivolous companionship. I had also put my religion on a backseat. Two years ago, tired of the battles in my mind, I turned to my holy book. As I read the first couple of pages, I felt a peace descend upon my heart and a rationality I had not been able to summon up until then. Images that would constantly be hovering in my tired mind began to rest. Eventually, they started receding, as I began to read more and more from the scripture every day. Pain changed into reason. It became my strength and solace. I started turning to it to reverse every single mistake, or to fulfil every wish. Finally, I grew tired of turning to it with every desperation. There was also the knowledge that the desperation was often a result of my own failings. One day, I put it reverently aside. I told myself I was not forsaking it, but I needed to find my own strength and rationality. I needed to break the vicious cycle of pain that I knew I had been responsible for. I was tired of asking questions, being shown the way, and then failing again.

I was getting drawn towards that universe which would change my life. My life was progressing on the path that would lead me exactly where I was supposed to go. We do not realize how things come together that way; how sometimes pain and misfortune take us to where we are supposed to end up all along.

1

The Beginning of the
Journey of Self-realization

❧❀☙

Day Zero

My son is away at boarding school. I have arranged for my daughter to be dropped to my mother's. I have washed her hair. I will remember its lustre with the strongest yearning in the coming days. I pick up my small bag. It contains very little. I feel like a sick person on her way to a rest and recuperation centre.

I am calm during the drive. As we leave the city behind, the surroundings become greener. The mystic Aravali hills come into sight; they are desert hills, steeped in culture. On a narrower road close to the ashram, I see people trudging slowly towards the ashram with bags slung over their shoulders. It is far too hot to be walking on this dusty road. I feel a tremor of apprehension. I had expected luxury cars and glamorous women wanting to explore the realm of renunciation and peace.

The ashram is nondescript. Apart from a few people standing near two tables placed together, there is not much activity. We park the car and enter the gate. No one is telling anyone what to do. I head towards what looks like an office.

After a whispered conversation with the lady inside, I am handed a form and told to fill it up.

My daughter is getting restless. I register the thought vaguely at the back of my mind. I am given a key with a number. I ask where I have to deposit my cash and phone, and the lady points to a room opposite the office. The man there is gruff. He takes my phone and the money and puts it in an envelope.

My husband heads out of the gate to take a call on his phone. I notice a little table with biscuits and tea placed on it. I long for a cup of tea but am unsure whether we can help ourselves. Just then, a kind looking man strolls by and tells my daughter to help herself to some biscuits. She picks up a handful and hands one to me. I eat it because I have been told that the last meal here is at five in the evening and it is past five now. I am used to eating little meals throughout the day and am scared of being hungry.

At a short distance from the main gate, I see the temple-like, evocative structure which I have been dreaming of seeing. It is the pagoda, where I will pray and find my liberation. I can hardly wait. I wrongly assume that we will be staying in it and I start heading towards it, but my husband points to a sign on the right side of the walkway which reads 'FEMALE RESIDENCES'. I am a little baffled. We head down that path. Branches of trees intertwined overhead give the place a cooler feel in the hot and sultry weather of August. It is evening and though the sun has lost its awesome power of the day, it is still very warm, and even the gentler rays prick the skin. The path underfoot is mossy and green. I spot monkeys in the distance. Then I hear peacocks and my heart thrills. Peacocks, for me, are symbolic of faith and hope and serenity.

We approach a hall to our left. A sign on it reads 'DINNING HALL'. Apparently, no one has paid much attention to details of the grammatical kind. We walk on. The path now slopes upwards. There is an overgrown field to our left and a triangular walkway up ahead. We pass two young women who are in animated conversation with each other. I am glad to see them. We soon come to a block at the end of the path, which has an open courtyard with rooms on three sides. It has a shabby and forlorn look. I shudder. My room is in the left corner of the courtyard. I open the door with my key. It is a dingy cell, about eight feet by ten and has only a tiny cot and a plastic chair. There are two stone slabs fixed into the wall. A narrow window overlooks an overgrown patch at the back of the block. This is to be my home for the next eleven days. My heart sinks a little, but it is the austerity I expected and an austerity which will cleanse my soul.

My daughter is nervous. I would have been too, were I at the tender age of seven and leaving my mother in a strange and intimidating place. But this thought only strikes me later. She tries to coerce me to take her last biscuit and in her haste to offer it, she drops a few crumbs on to the cracked cement floor of the cell. My husband admonishes her and with frustration stemming from my nervousness, I kneel in front of her and fold my hands in a gesture of supplication, pleading with her to give me a little peace of mind. It is an action I shall regret greatly afterwards. Tears form in her eyes. We head back to the main area near the office. Once there, we again do not know what to do. A notice I had not seen before tells us dinner will be at seven and that this will be followed by a meeting. Lights will be out at half past nine.

I am scared now at the thought of saying goodbye. I wonder if I can't just leave; just turn back and go back home to my trials and tribulations. My husband and daughter linger around uncertainly, not wanting to leave either, though dusk is approaching fast. It is like a scene from a slow silent film. The three protagonists stand in silence, frozen in a frame; not wanting the film to advance further.

I decide to take charge before panic gets the better of me, I tell my husband to leave as they have a long way to go. I sound more confident and cheerful than I feel, mostly for the benefit of my little girl. He asks me if I am sure and gives me a half hug; in this place, overt displays of affection seem out of place. My daughter clings to me while he goes to get the car. When he returns, she buries her face in my tummy and lets out the most horrible sound I have heard in years; a sound of keening; a sound arising from the innermost depths of her being. I steel myself, even though I too have tears behind my sunglasses. I swallow them, take off my glasses and put them on her face. I know she loves to wear them. I tell her to take them with her, as I will have no need for them here. She does not let go of me. I then tell her that the sight of her crying will make me unhappy after she leaves. She wipes off her tears, even though the anguish is visible in her eyes. My husband takes hold of her hand and leads her away. With a sinking feeling, I watch her stricken face in the car till it rolls out of sight. I am now truly alone to face the ordeals which will set me free. I start to weep silently. This is a strange and forbidding place and I have no idea what to expect for the next eleven days.

With cold dread in my heart, I turn around. A man is standing nearby and he smiles gently; the first smile from anyone in this place. I am grateful. He asks me if this is my first time and I nod. He tells me his daughter is a *sevika* – a helper – in this place and that she will be serving us. Not quite understanding the concept of a sevika in this place, where we will not be speaking to anyone, I nod again. He can sense my anguish and he does not say anything else. As I walk towards the room, I come upon three women standing together. I smile self-consciously at them. They smile broadly in turn and the oldest asks me if this is my first time. I nod and they tell me they are first-timers too. The ice is broken. I feel a little better. It is my first meeting with what will be my sisterhood.

There is a girl who I will just refer to as the American, who says she has been in India for only a day prior to coming here. Another is a thin girl who I will call N. The third is elderly, with two gold studs on either side of her nose. At that moment in time, we are four women who are bound by the common fact that we have all come to the ashram seeking something: refuge, or understanding, or something else. There are no barriers of age or nationality. I feel my apprehensions and doubts melting. These are also lost and frightened souls. We exchange more information about ourselves. N is married to a much older man and has a son. I wonder why the age difference is mentioned. The American is a bit nervous and self-conscious, but she hides it well with bright conversation and smiles. I tell my new friends that I have two children and that I am a writer. The writer bit brings about many exclamations of admiration.

A few minutes later, we are approached by two young girls, who also ask if we are first-timers. I wonder at the fact that this question is uppermost in everyone's minds. One of the girls is particularly attractive and her manner is direct and less self-conscious. She does not smile as freely as the others. I learn that she is studying architecture in Milan. Henceforth, I will refer to her as the Italian. There are two pairs of silver studs in her beautifully shaped ears. I will gaze at them often during the course of the stay here.

As we are talking, a tall, lean girl walks confidently past us, pulling a suitcase behind her as she does so. She is wearing high heels and they make a loud, clicking sound.

We stand and gossip and titter like children, trying to overcome our apprehension and nervousness. Someone points out that it is time for us to head towards the dining hall for supper. Already the sombre atmosphere of the place is descending upon us. All of us experience mostly the same thoughts and feelings in similar situations, so I assume the others feel the same. By the time we approach the dining hall, the American, N and I have ended up together and the others have formed little groups of their own. N is sharing personal details of her life with me. It is uncomfortable for me, a virtual stranger, to be privy to it, but sensing a deep despair within her, I listen politely.

The dining hall is spartan. It has rows of steel-topped tables with plastic chairs. N and I sit together. A long table to a side has large containers of food on it. Three women are standing behind the table. The food is simple, as I had expected, but wholesome. I take a rather generous second helping, to stave off expected hunger pangs.

N tells me she is worried that she may lose track of days here. I realize I have been worrying about the same thing. I have left my watch at home, expecting that we would not be allowed to wear it, although most others still have theirs on and are also sporting many items of jewellery.

Since we are not allowed to have any reading or writing material on us, the only way I can probably remember what day it is, is to etch lines on the wall of my cell, a la Papillon. It is only a half jocular thought. Without any access to the basic things we take for granted in our daily lives, everything here will take on a different magnitude and level of difficulty. It is like going back in time and learning how to adapt to survive.

We are required to wash our own utensils here. An inner room has a long tiled basin and four huge steel racks above for the plates, bowls, spoons and glasses. No one tells us what to do; it is either instinctive or done by imitating others. It is strange how much we can understand and communicate without using words. Later, I will mull on the fact that we use far too many words in our daily lives, most of them unnecessary.

There is still time before we are to assemble for the meeting, so I bolt to my room to use the washroom. When I return, the dining hall looks very different. The long blue curtain, which partitioned the dining hall into separate eating areas for women and men, has been drawn aside. We now sit together, although in two separate groups. Most of the women are fidgeting and speaking in hushed whispers. The men are quieter. I am in the row closest to the group of men and suddenly I am conscious of the big and bold tattoo on my right ankle.

A big man with a considerable pot belly appears and starts addressing the congregation, explaining some basic guidelines regarding our stay. He tells us to deposit our valuables, phones and reading and writing material with the management, although this must already have been done by all.

He then switches on an audio tape. The man who speaks in the recording has a funny accent. He tells us five precepts we are supposed to observe during our stay: a vow of silence, a vow not to tell lies, a vow not to steal, a vow not to kill or harm and a vow of celibacy. He tells us we should not harm any living thing here, whether it is a snake or a scorpion and I see a few women shuddering. I wonder briefly if this is a forewarning of dangerous creatures in the area, but I do not have any great phobia of little creatures and my attention soon shifts to observing the congregation from the corner of my eye. Most of the women seem from humble backgrounds and are dressed very simply. It is the same with the men.

The pot-bellied man switches off the tape and asks if we have any questions. The men have a few, but they seem unimportant and silly. An old woman gets up and asks obsequiously if she should deposit the notepad and pen that she has in her purse, even though she will not be using it. I expect the pot-bellied man to admonish her for still having it upon her person but he just patiently and half smilingly asks what will happen if she wants to note down something from Guruji's discourses. She says she will not write anything and he shrugs in acquiescence.

He then introduces the sevikas and the sevaks: the women and men who will be looking after our material needs during our stay. The sevikas stand up as they are being introduced, but look disinterested and cold. The sevaks, on the other hand, fold their hands in a respectful namaste.

The pot-bellied man calls out our seat numbers for the meditation hall, after which we are asked to go there for meditation. A sevak starts speaking out the numbers in a loud and clear voice, but the sevika assigned for the job speaks in hushed whispers, as if she has just emerged from several years of solitary meditation. The women are getting confused and irritable and one sitting at the back jumps up and volunteers to read out the numbers. Chaos prevails, but all finally manage to get their numbers. I look forward to the vow of silence which will finally isolate me from any conversation.

I assume incorrectly that the meditation will be in the beautiful white pagoda. The meditation hall is an unlovely building. It has small steps leading to a door with fly-proofing. Inside, there are square shaped cushions neatly arranged in rows over mats throughout the hall. It feels intimidating and forbidding, but there is an atmosphere of piety.

We have been allotted seat numbers along with our room key tags. There are cardboard counters placed next to each cushion for identification. There is no need for conversation or questioning.

We sit down on the smaller cushions placed atop the larger ones. There are soothing uplighters in the corners and a raised platform in front where a man and a woman are seated in chairs draped with white cloth. As in the dining hall, the men and women are segregated into two groups on each side of the hall. I assume the man and woman on the platform are our guides or teachers.

The male teacher introduces himself in fluent English. The female teacher does not speak. He introduces her and explains that questions from female students will be put to the female teacher while the questions from male students will be addressed to him.

The American and the Italian have seats close to mine. I feel safe and secure. The American is sitting diagonally ahead. She has struck the pose of a *yogini*: cross-legged, with her hands on her knees, the fingers curled upwards. I strike the same pose. I am ready for instruction and emancipation.

The male teacher announces that our Guru will give us instructions on what needs to be done. He also switches on an audio tape and we hear the same voice that we heard in the dining room. There is a funny drawl in the voice and the accent is very similar to that of a well-known male comedian in Hindi cinema. Guruji speaks first in Hindi and then in English for non-Hindi speaking students and tells us that the five precepts are the *sīla* or foundation of the course and that without these, our meditation and introspection will be incomplete. I have no problem with the implementation of any of these, though I do raise my eyebrows at the celibacy bit. He then instructs us to observe our breath. He tells us this is the technique given by Gautama, the Buddha. The way he pronounces Gautama makes me smile.

Following his instructions, I try to observe my breathing, but I realize to my annoyance that I simply cannot focus on it for more than a second or two. In the first few minutes, I become aware of the diversity and rapidity of our thoughts and how little control we have over our minds.

As I am still struggling with trying to focus, Guruji starts singing some *dohas* or verses. He has an unmelodious voice and I am surprised he sings so un-self consciously. His voice vibrates on the last syllable in a very strange manner and ends in groans. I do not know what to make of this Guruji with his strange accent, peculiar pronunciation and groans.

By the time the audio ends, I am very tired. I look forward to retiring to my room. Night has fallen by the time we emerge from the hall. Crickets have started their cacophony. We walk back from the hall to our rooms. We are all acutely conscious now of the vow of silence. A deep quiet has descended, but I am not afraid of silence or solitude.

N and I are in the same block. It is not going to be of much consequence. The other women I have come to know head towards the block adjoining ours. Just as we enter the courtyard, we are accosted by a horde of huge grasshoppers, who have decided to hold their festivities around the ghostly white light of the lamp post in the middle of the courtyard. I am repulsed and frightened, but continue walking; hoping the grasshoppers won't jump on me before I reach the safety of my room. One unfortunately descends on N and she screams. I do not attempt to help and she runs to her room.

There are three or four huge grasshoppers on my door. I flick them away with my handkerchief, conscious of the fact that we are not supposed to harm any creature. Opening the door, I rush inside and bolt it, heaving silently. It is frightening and lonely in my room with the single dim bulb. As I scan the room for grasshoppers and other creatures, I spy a mat under the cot. I jam it against the bottom of the door to block the space under it.

Not wanting to think too much, I quickly wash my face in the little bathroom, brush my teeth, change into my night clothes and slip into bed. I hope to fall asleep soon to escape the cavalcade of thought and be fresh for the start of meditation tomorrow morning at half past four. I wonder how I will get up in the morning as I do not have a watch or phone, but I am certain the ashram people will not let us sleep away the meditation periods. There is a wall clock directly in front of my room, near the entrance to the courtyard and am extremely glad for it. At least I will have some idea of time.

I drift away to sleep with thoughts of expectation mingled with thoughts of oppression.

2

THE LONELY QUEST

Day One

At four in the morning, somewhere in the distance, a bell rings as softly as a spoon tapping on crystal. It is rung slowly four times, as if there is no hurry in the world and all is at peace. I like the sound. I am a morning person. The energy I have in the morning is unsurpassed by that at any other time of the day and I cherish those quiet moments when everyone else is asleep and I can think without interruption while sipping on my tea.

This hour of morning, however, is an unearthly hour to wake and I do not have my cup of tea. I long briefly for it, but my mind is charged in anticipation. I hurriedly brush, comb my shoulder-length hair and then put it up. Meditation is serious business, not an indulgence of vanity. I change into calf-length pants and a comfortable T-shirt and slip into my black flip-flops. At ten minutes past four, the sevika of our block raps loudly on our doors and calls out for us to wake up. Suddenly, the low clamour of early morning chores can be heard. The soft bell in the distance rings four times again. We have been told that it will announce ten minutes remain to reach the meditation hall. Soon after, there is a violent tinkling of a hand bell in the courtyard. The sevikas are apparently equipped with hand bells, which

26

aid the door banging. However, it also has a pleasant sound and I wonder if all things out here are designed to be soft and mellifluous.

I set off in the dark along with a few others. No one walks together. The sevika is already near the hall, ushering everyone in with swift, emphatic gestures. I wonder why she is so excitable. We troop in and take our assigned places. The meditation hall is stuffy. But the atmosphere is soothing, with ambient light suited to this time of morning. We assume the cross-legged pose and start the same practice of observing our breaths. No-one tells us what to do. We are now acting on instinct and observation.

The door of the hall has whiney hinges. The stragglers disturb the silence each time it is opened. This will be very trying in the future, when the need for absolute concentration will be combined with pain. My eyes are open, observing people in the immediate vicinity. After a while, they close slowly. Suddenly, my concentration becomes more focused. As last night, though, I cannot focus for more than a couple of seconds before my mind strays. The more I try and rein it in, the more wayward thoughts cross my mind. It seems I am not even the one doing the thinking. My mind apparently has a will of its own. Sitting cross-legged is painful and uncomfortable and I unfold my legs every few minutes. The hall is deathly quiet now, with everyone struggling unsuccessfully with their minds.

Surprisingly, I am cold. The night chill had not yet been dissipated by the warm rays of the morning sun. This disturbs my concentration greatly and I long for something to cover my arms and my calves. I think longingly of the long-sleeved T-shirt in my bag, which I put in just in case I felt cold at some point during the course, though it was unexpected in the warm weather of August.

I lose track of time. I do not know how much time has passed when the male teacher, who has been sitting silently on the platform and meditating like the rest of us, announces that it is time to head to the dining hall for breakfast.

We walk slowly towards the dining hall. I am shivering, even though gentle rays of sunshine are now filtering through the trees. I take off my footwear outside the dining hall and place it carefully on the shoe rack. Breakfast is sumptuous; chickpeas and porridge, bananas and sprouts and a choice of milk or tea. I do not really need the tea, awake and alert as I am and I settle for the hot, sweet milk instead. I do not remember when was the last time I had hot milk in the sultry weather of August, but it is early in the morning and the stillness of meditation has cooled my body. I deliberately choose not to sit next to anyone I know. A huge cooler is on in the dining hall and the draught is chilly and uncomfortable. I decide to ask the sevika for a blanket for the night. We are allowed to talk to the sevikas if we require anything, but obviously, such interactions have to be kept to a minimum.

I approach the sevika and whisper to her that I need a blanket. In the typical Indian manner, she repeats my demand in the form of a question. I nod and tell her I was cold last night. I wonder if she thinks I am odd.

I wash my utensils in the long sink and ignore the American and N as if we are strangers. N has a distinct gait I have come to recognize from a distance; it is slow and swaying, as if she is immersed in deep thought. There is a water cooler outside the dining hall; I fill cold water into my plastic bottle. It feels weighty in my hands as I walk up the sloping path from the dining hall towards the residential blocks. The morning is beautiful, but I am terribly sleepy now.

When I reach my block, I am greeted with a sight which fills me with delight and hope. A peacock is perched on the top of the courtyard, fanning its tail feathers. It does not seem to be frightened by the sight of the approaching women. I linger outside the block, scared to disturb the peacock in its display of love. When I walk into the courtyard, the peacock obligingly turns around, so I can again see its beautiful tail spread out.

I don't really feel like going inside the room. I peer at a time-table that is pinned onto a bulletin board on a wall of the courtyard. We have time until eight, when the next meditation session begins. It is about quarter past seven. With a sigh of relief and longing, I head towards my room to sleep. I assume we are free to do what we want in the time we are not in the meditation hall. I enter my room, flop on to my bed and am asleep within seconds. Within ten or fifteen minutes, however, I am rudely awakened by the sevika who raps loudly on my door. Jolted out of my slumber, I quickly rise to open it. She asks if I was sleeping and before I can answer, admonishes me slightly. She is carrying an old, coarse blanket, which she hands over to me. She then suggests that I utilize this time to bathe. I nod my head, not at all inclined to make any unnecessary conversation. She turns around and walks away.

I do not want to flout rules, so I start folding the bedclothes. Just then, I notice a big lizard on the wall. I almost faint with revulsion. Although not really scared of lizards, I do not appreciate them in such close vicinity. Fortified with the knowledge that I am a meditator who is supposed to be calm under all situations and deal with them wisely, I realize I have to get it out of my room.

There are three clothes hangers on hooks in my room. I hurriedly take one off and tap it on the wall close to the lizard, trying to make it go towards the door. It darts in the opposite direction. It is now higher up and I realize I need something longer. My brain feels sharper. I am thinking very fast now. I shall improvise. I feel almost invincible. There is nothing in the room, no stick or handle or anything. I push open the bathroom door and spy a dirty toilet brush. The thought of picking it up makes me queasy. But there is no choice. I brandish it about on the wall on which the lizard is resting, looking wary now. The brush is wet. Droplets fly off it and onto my face. I am nauseated, but I do not abandon the mission. I tap the brush on the wall to make the lizard move. It moves closer and closer to the door and finally, it slips into the gap at the top and is gone. Not content with chasing it out of my room, I step out and run after it, though I have left the toilet brush in the room, lest the others think I'm crazy.

N is watching from her doorway. Apparently, I have been making enough noise to attract attention. I do not smile, or give any explanation. I am terribly relieved and proud of my courage.

I fold the blanket neatly and place it on the stone slab. It might be bug-infested. Then, with great trepidation, I decide to clean the bathroom. I am just about done when the bell starts ringing. The sevika, who seems unconvinced that we can make it to the meditation hall on our own, breezes all over the courtyard with her little bell. I lock my room and as I walk towards the meditation hall, I notice a good deal of washing is hanging from the two nylon ropes strung across the courtyard. I am surprised to see it. It's only the first day!

In less than a day, our walk seems to have become an unhurried gait with small steps. Already, we seem a little different from the beings of yesterday. We take our places in the hall. I look around as we wait. The teachers are sitting like statues on the platform. After everyone has settled down, the male teacher switches on the audio tape. There are no rebukes or instructions; just an expectation that everyone will be on time for meditation in the hall. Sometimes, the sevika will be sent out to look for absentees, but even then, no words will be spoken: the teacher will gesticulate with her eyes and the sevika will quickly understand what needs to be done.

Today, Guruji tells us that observing is the path to untie the knots we have formed in this life and in previous lifetimes. He also gently warns us to not be disappointed if we cannot train our minds immediately because it is the most difficult thing in the world to try and control our thoughts. He tells us to continue observing respiration.

The Italian and American seem to already be deep in concentration. I gaze at the beautiful silver studs on the Italian's ears. She also sits diagonally ahead of me on the right side. However, after a while, my eyes once again close automatically, as if the wise and benign part of my mind is telling me to shut out the sights and sounds of the world.

My thoughts are totally awry and out of control. They mostly centre on pain and anguish, but do not necessarily stay there. They go way back in the past, they project madly into the future, they conjure up situations and they plunge into dreams. They soar with joy and then are thrown into darkness. They are never still. They defy logic and sequence and reality and dance madly around hope and fear, desire and dread.

I can still barely observe my breath for more than two seconds. It seems like a losing battle. The sound of glass bangles and other jewellery as the women shift in their places adds to the distraction. After about an hour, the male teacher announces that we can rest for five minutes. I stretch out my legs with my knees bent and feet flat on the floor. Some women stretch out on their backs. A few head out of the hall. The sevika goes up quietly to the women lying down and points towards the platform on which the teachers sit. She whispers to N, who is lying almost supine, that we cannot stretch out our legs towards the platform. I can hear her because it is so quiet and N sits right in front of me. There is no religious or divine symbol on the platform and this kind of meditation does not seem to have religious connotations, so I wonder why she says this.

After the short break, the meditation starts again. My legs have started to hurt. In India, there are numerous ceremonies and rituals which require one to sit cross-legged on the ground for hours at a time, but I do not remember it ever causing so much agony. After what seems like another hour, the teacher tells us we can either go to our rooms to meditate or continue meditating in the hall. Most of us get up gladly. The sevika is standing at the door with the whiney hinges and she looks at the departing women as if they are her vulnerable flock. I decide to bring up the matter of the bangles with her. She looks surprised and uncomfortable and mumbles something incoherently. I wonder why this violation does not evoke a stronger response.

Once in my room, I climb on to my bed to meditate, forsaking the old mat for the comparative softness of the hard bed. After the thick, firm cushions of the meditation hall, I cannot imagine sitting cross-legged on a thin mat on the floor; and it shall forever be consigned to its sole role of blocking the space under the door. Leaning back slightly against the wall, I muse how we were not given any time to adjust to the hardships of the course. A loud knocking on my door startles me out of my reverie. I jump up and open the door. It is once again the sevika, who tells me the doors must be left open.

There is no escaping the sevika and her interruptions at my attempts for silence and solitude. I cannot argue with her, but I feel we could meditate better with some privacy. Women are still walking about outside; one is noisily unlocking her door, another is putting something outside her room and a third is popping out her head from her door. Perplexed, I return to the bed and close my eyes.

After what must have been a few minutes of meditation, I open my eyes to see if the others have retreated inside their rooms for meditation. N is shuffling outside her room. Her eyes are on me and in that split fraction of a second, I think

I see envy. Is she envying my determination and outwardly peaceful and calm demeanour? Guilty of having seen her watching me, I hurriedly close my eyes.

I am getting drowsy. I try and will myself to be alert, but I cannot control the waves of drowsiness and I finally succumb to temptation. Just before I fall asleep, I sigh both resignedly and contentedly in the comforting knowledge that one cannot fight fate. Just now, I do not care if the sevika breaks down my door and shames me in front of the entire block.

I sleep for no more than half an hour. My body clock is getting attuned to time without a watch. I wake at half past ten. There is half an hour to go before lunch. Feeling very guilty, I get back into sitting position on the bed with the wall as a backrest and start meditating.

I am glad when it is eleven o'clock and time for lunch. Lunch is as sumptuous as breakfast. I go for second helpings as usual. I look at no-one in the hall, though I can feel a few eyes on me.

After lunch, I head back to the room to bathe. Lizard droppings are stuck on the joints of the walls in the bathroom and around the window. They make me queasy. I am glad for the little mirror above the sink and as I gaze at myself in it, I notice tiny red bumps on my belly. These must be bug bites; they are too big to be mosquito bites. I grumble silently to myself. I am vaguely conscious of the fact that we must not talk even to ourselves. No one has told us this; in fact, most of the rights and wrongs and dos and don'ts occur to me instinctively. I will mull on the merits of this but also realize how their not being communicated or enforced also decides who experiences what reality through different levels of comprehension and dedication.

I have enough time before the next meditation period, which starts at one. It is barely half past eleven. I do not have much to do, so I start moisturizing my body slowly. In the isolation of the ashram, I feel like my own beloved. It is a strange feeling.

That chore finished, I comb my hair and tie it up once again. I fold the clothes I had worn in the morning and put them inside the bag. I then step out, keen to explore my surroundings. There does not seem to be anyone about. The path ends at the dining hall. I deliberately turn right towards the pagoda. It has enchanted me ever since I came here and I want to see it closely.

It is only a short distance from the meditation hall. I furtively look around, but it is afternoon now and very warm and no one is around. I tell myself that the worst that can happen is a rebuke and I carry on down the hedge-lined path that leads to it. The hedge is untrimmed and is a good screen. I am filled with reverence and awe when I reach the entrance. It does not seem to be the main entrance. There is a sign on it which says 'female entrance'. So that's alright. At least I'm not entering forbidden male area.

'Female entrance' sounds a little anatomical; I reflect subconsciously, as I open the glass doors of the pagoda, shivering with excitement. I am entering a sacred realm, full of forbidden secrets. I am in a foyer, bare of any furnishing. It is cool here, which is to be expected, since I have just come in from the harsh afternoon sun. There is a notice board and two stone slabs, presumably for footwear. A list of names is on the board, with cell numbers in front of the names. I wonder why the list does not have my name.

There is another glass door in front of me. I open it and enter inside. It is dark inside. There are some steps leading up. Fading arrows on the walls depict the numbering of the cells. I cannot make out the layout at all, though I can view some cells on the left side, above the steps. There is a passage to the right of where I am standing. Though a little apprehensive, I slowly walk down the passage. It is lined with cells on the right side. It all looks very dismal. Gingerly,

I swing open the door to the cell nearest to me. It is nothing but a tiny room, approximately six feet by six, with cushions similar to the ones in the main meditation hall. There is a little circular opening high above, with spokes on it like those on a wheel. A little light filters through it into the cell, which is eerie and claustrophobic and I wonder why my friend advised me to meditate in the pagoda whenever I could.

Having seen the cells, I retrace my steps back to the entrance. A peahen is standing just outside the doors and it quickly scampers away. I walk back along the path. It is almost one o'clock and I am one of the first few people to enter the hall. I dread sitting down for hours but welcome the challenge of controlling my mind.

When the audio tape is switched on, Guruji tells us that observing our breaths is the way to take out defilements from the deep recesses of our minds. This excites me, but the pain in my legs is getting more severe with every hour of meditation and it is very hard to concentrate.

In the break, I see that others also seem to be in the throes of pain. No one is sitting cross-legged anymore. Some meditators go out, while others sit hunched over with their legs stretched out. I sit vacantly. I have barely been able to relax my body when the male teacher switches on the tape again.

There is nothing I can do but try and focus on my breath. But I notice now that my thoughts are not quite as diverse and lightning quick as before. It's like my mind has quietened down a little. But there is also something else. There are songs playing in my head; old songs from a bygone era of Hindi films. I wonder at the strangeness of this fact. But I cannot turn them off and they do not really seem to be interfering with the meditation.

Another change is taking place. My thoughts are getting concentrated to the present and to my immediate surroundings. I think more about the other meditators here, our daily schedule and the peacocks. My thoughts are converging onto the little area of the ashram.

I now step out in breaks and drink lustily from my bottle. It is very hot outside in the scorching sun, but I do not drink just because I am thirsty. There is nothing else to do. We stand outside, vacantly. We group together in the cooler areas in the recess. Everyone walks very slowly, almost shuffling along, with N being the worst. She looks as if she is going to fall while walking. I try not to observe people, but when the object of one's attention is at a distance, it naturally falls into the periphery of one's vision. The others do not seem to have any qualms about observing and watching others. I can feel their gaze upon me. The sevika's eyes are also never averted and it makes me very uncomfortable.

I head for the toilets in the next break. They are built underground, with stone steps leading down to them. The steps are littered with leaves. There are two sinks with mirrors in the toilets. I look for traces of anguish in my face but I cannot find any. My eyes are clear and calm as I watch my reflection dispassionately.

The cubicles are to the left and I gingerly open one. The toilet is nothing but a shallow bed-pan shaped opening in the floor. Thankfully, it is clean and there isn't any pungent or offensive smell.

It is back to the hall. Guruji tells us not to be disappointed if our minds 'wander away', like a creature with legs. I smile inwardly. It is still very difficult to focus on breathing. A kaleidoscope of imagery is always in the background, even if there are no active thoughts to disturb the concentration. Sounds also distract the mind constantly, even if they do not translate into thoughts.

The songs have ceased. In their place, the famed and revered chant, the *Gayatri Mantra* has taken over. I wonder at this strange occurrence, because I had never learnt the chant! It fades away on its own after a while. With no songs or mantras in my head now, I start chanting silently, 'breath in, breath out', with each inhalation and exhalation. It focuses my attention better.

It has been eight or nine hours of meditation since last night and my body is revolting at the inhumane treatment I am subjecting it to. Even though I change positions frequently, it does not alleviate the pain. Sitting erect is also taking its toll. In one of the breaks, two women, who are probably as exhausted as I am, go and sit with their backs to a wall. I look enviously at them, but I am determined to not cave in to frailty.

Finally, it is time for tea. In the dining hall, I fill up my plate with puffed rice and pick up a glass of hot, sweet milk. There is nothing else to eat. Surprisingly, I am not really hungry. Thoughts of anguish, bereavement, unhappiness and helplessness course through my mind, but so do those of pride, accomplishment and hope. I know I am on an astounding journey of discovery.

I have also started observing everything around me closely and trying to consign it to memory. My stay at the ashram just might make an interesting subject for my first book.

Upon reaching my room, I am suddenly overwhelmed by pain and tiredness and I climb on to my bed. Placing my hands on the ledge of the window which faces the overgrown patch at the back, I lower my chin onto them. Suddenly, the loneliness and pain I have tried to ignore since yesterday overcomes me and I start crying with desperate silent sobs. I am appalled at the tears. I am here to find strength. I have been very stoic and brave so far, handling fairly well the loneliness, the isolation, the grief inside and the physical agony of meditation. But I am also glad for the tears. I want to rid my soul of some of the black, bleak despair within. I feel violated, claustrophobic and lost. I long to be comforted and held, and for someone to listen to my story. N is five steps away. I need companionship like a physical ache. I am very tempted to go to her and pour out my grief. I know she will comfort me. But I cannot. I will not break the vow of silence and resilience. I get up to go wash my face.

There isn't much to do in the room, especially in the evening after tea. The day is winding up. I shall remember it as the mellowest and most comforting part of day. Only an hour and a half of meditation remains. I am looking forward to the audio-visual discourse in the evening. My friend has told me it is very interesting. Any distraction from this painful and agonizing routine will definitely be welcome.

We are cloistered in an area which is scarcely bigger than a park, but it is very serene and I feel closer to Nature than ever before. There really isn't much here to overtly delight the senses, but it is a microcosm of a beautiful and ideal world; a world that is soothing and wondrous in its simplicity. I love the peacocks, which are always foraging around in the undergrowth, or calling from branches of trees. Sometimes, they look at me quizzically, forgetting that they are not creatures of thought. Beauty is abundant in the tiny bugs and worms and the different shapes and colours of plants. I also search for a peacock feather all the time. It will be my talisman, my own 'white feather'. Every day, when I walk on the path, I examine the area bordering it. But it is overgrown with a profusion of lush green shrubs and weeds, verdant and fresh because of the late monsoon.

In the hall, there are many empty seats on the women's side. The teachers are already in and sitting unmoving in their seats. I sit down on my cushion and close my eyes. The vision of a gigantic nose appears and it feels like I am observing respiration in that image before my closed eyes. Once again, I am in the world between reality and fantasy.

The male teacher puts on the audio tape. The player clicks very loudly each time it is switched on or off. I wonder why it has not been replaced by something more modern.

Guruji now says something different from the usual exhortation to observe breath. He says to try and feel sensations on the nose and on the philtrum, the area above the upper lip. These new instructions promise to break the monotony of observing simple breathing but I do not know how to go about feeling any sensation on such a tiny area.

However, as I valiantly keep trying to feel sensations in this area, I slowly became aware of very feeble scratchy sensations on my nose. The new discovery makes time pass faster and after what seems to be only a short while, the teacher announces rest. He also informs us of something I already know about: the audio-visual after the break, in which Guruji would explain the technique. The Hindi discourse, he says, will be held in the meditation hall, whereas the English one will be held in the 'mini hall'. My friend has already advised that I would be more comfortable watching the English discourse.

I have seen a room next to the dining hall marked 'MINI *DHAMMA* HALL' and I guess correctly that that is where I need to head. It is dusk now and a little strange to be heading towards the dining hall at this time. I see the old lady with the gold nose studs, N, the American and the tall girl who had walked in with heels at the beginning of the course outside the mini hall. The hall is open and the light is on but no one is around. Like an uncertain little flock of sheep, we quietly walk in and sit down on the cushions placed there. There are two rows of them on one side and two more rows across the room. Two cushions are against the wall at the back and they are quickly occupied by the old lady and another girl who I notice for the first time. My body and legs are still revolting and I ache to also slump against the wall.

There is a small old television set in front. I mentally berate myself for not having packed my spectacles in my bag. My eyes are already tired and hurting; maybe gazing inwards is as strenuous as gazing outside. There is a row of windows on the wall in front and I can see the silhouetted branches and leaves of a tree. A broad pillar stands in the middle of the hall, like a sentinel separating the two genders of mankind. The hall is dim and we sit in absolute silence; seven women in their own private worlds; isolated from the rest of humanity. It is a strange and eerie feeling. One could have heard a feather drop. I muse at the kind of patience and silence we have already acquired in one day. If we want, we can look at each other and smile, or gesticulate or even communicate silently about our puzzlement, but we all do nothing but look ahead at the blank television set. We are as disjointed from each other as complete strangers.

I am surprised that there are so few of us here for the English discourse. There are no men present. But just then, a lone man walks in from an entrance on the other side of the mini-hall. He is middle-aged and bespectacled. He is followed by another man who walks in briskly and strides purposefully towards the television. He switches it on and the audio-visual starts.

I finally see the face of Guruji, our teacher, who instructs us in his funny accent in the main meditation hall. He is sitting down cross-legged on some kind of platform. Seated next to him is his wife; the relationship evident from her patient, homely demeanour, the bindi on her forehead and the manner in which they sit comfortably together. Both are dressed very simply. I know of the family which Guruji hails from: it is a prominent industrialist family of India. I am surprised at the path he has chosen, of worldly good, rather than worldly gains. Guruji is portly and with his neatly combed, sparse hair and crisp buttoned-up shirt, he looks nothing like a traditional Guru.

His voice sounds different in the audio visual. He starts by saying the first day is always difficult, because our bodies and minds are prisoners of fixed patterns and start revolting the moment the pattern is tampered with. He says many realities pertaining to our physical structure will surface in the next few days and we will realize that the breath is related to the mind by discovering what happens when the mind loses its balance in times of stress or anger. He says the practice of observing sensations has already started making our minds more sensitive and sharp.

Guruji says we have unintentionally started knowing the mind through the discovery of its fickleness and lack of sequence or logic. He says it would be impossible to keep a diary of the many thoughts that go through it for even a few seconds. I reflect at how true this is. There are too many spontaneous thoughts even in a single second. It is, he continues, maddening to try and rein in those thoughts. They swing between two fields of thought: past memory and the unseen future. The past is recreated constantly through memory, for example, we dwell upon past sorrows or pain and keep conjuring up future scenarios involving it.

I have also been letting my pain dictate a future I cannot determine. How hard we make it for ourselves!

Our mind, Guruji elaborates, does not want to live in the present and that is why it remains so agitated all the time. It keeps oscillating between the two realms of pleasant and unpleasant thoughts, which result in constant craving and aversion. However, he says, we must not be disappointed at this habit pattern and advises us to accept reality with equanimity. I am consoled by the fact that I am not alone in my difficult endeavour. We also must not, he says, use the aid of any mantra, chant or imagery to meditate, because although the mind becomes calmer when we focus on a word or an image, the goal is not to calm it, but to purify it by removing impurities at the 'root level'. I resolve to not allow any imagery or word to enter my mind henceforth.

Guruji says we tie knots inside us all the time because of the great attachment we have with our physical and mental structure and the 'I's that we define ourselves by. We should know ourselves not merely at the intellectual level, but at the experiential level, moving from the surface inwards, exploring the truth of the entire field of matter within our bodies. This excites me tremendously. I want to get to the subtlest truth. Why have I lived with self-inflicted pain? Why have I been melancholy's child? Why am I here, searching so desperately for liberation, while others lead their lives with much the same crests and troughs and no need for salvation and liberation?

The camera pans in jerkily to Guruji. His wife goes out of focus. I muse that the video has been shot in a rather amateur manner. Guruji says by knowing ourselves completely, we can realize the law of nature; the law that rewards us when we live in accordance with it and punishes us when we don't.

Now he tells us a little story to illustrate that we cannot experience or live someone else's reality or truth. It is one of the many simple stories we will hear in the next ten days. A man lives on one side of a river bank but longs to get to the other bank because of the wonderful things he has heard about it from others. However, in spite of the craving, he makes no effort to swim across and stays forever on his side of the river.

There are a few giggles when Guruji imitates the man in the story in a jocular manner and says, 'Oh other bank, please come here; I want to enjoy you.' I do not find this amusing, but I am glad for my soul sisters; I know that they are suffering like me and are also lost in their own worlds of fatigue, amazement, doubt, wonder and longing.

I get excited listening to the words 'the bank on the other side'. This could be the title of my book. I have already begun living the story I want to write about getting to a bank on the other side. I had no idea that meditation in a small ashram could yield such a spectrum of experiences.

Guruji carries on with the discourse. He says we spend our entire lives generating negativity and misery and making others miserable along with ourselves. The essence of life is thus lost. This meditation would teach us to be peaceful and harmonious within. He warns us though, that we would undergo a deep surgical operation of the mind, through which deep-rooted complexes would be released and that this would be a painful process.

The thought of a deep surgical operation of the mind which will free it of all its complexities makes me happy and hopeful. However, the part about pain being a necessary part of the process will be forgotten and I shall push myself almost to the brink in the next few days, trying only to push the limits of my endurance.

Guruji tells us many people leave the ashram, unable to bear the ordeal, especially on the second and the sixth day. This knowledge fills me with unease; it is the second day tomorrow. He talks about the determination we must have to brave the ordeals ahead. He then smiles and says we must meditate seriously in our residential quarters as well. I flush. Naughtily, he says we may think we are very smart and will not succumb to sleep, but would be snoring before we could realize our weakness. Everyone, including me, starts laughing. This is the first time that the tension and strain of the past twenty-four hours and really, of the last couple of months, leaves me. It feels good to laugh and it feels good to hear the embarrassment in our laughter. So I am not alone in my weaknesses, I smile inwardly, quite pleased with how things are progressing, even though my entire being quakes at the thought of the pain.

Guruji now advises us not eat more than we require. He seems to know all our weaknesses and follies. I have been overeating out of fear of being hungry. He also advises us to not move outside the demarcated area and stresses the importance of silence, as the reality within can only be manifested when we are completely focused only on our own being.

His voice becomes softer now and he tells us to rid ourselves of the bondages and shackles of ignorance and to find real happiness, real peace and real harmony. His words fill me with hope. I will understand the concept of real happiness, real peace and real harmony much later, when I am back to my world and confronted with choices giving me an option between short-lived joy and long-term happiness.

Guruji closes his eyes and raises his right hand in a gesture of benediction. The camera pans out and his wife comes into focus once again. He chants the words '*bhavatu sabba mangalam*' thrice. The third repetition ends in a quivering, drawn-out groan. Guruji clears his throat. Apparently, he has an audience in the recording, because there is a chanting of the word *sadhu* in response. Guruji explains that 'bhavatu sabba mangalam' means 'may all beings be happy' and sadhu means 'well said' or 'so be it'.

He then takes off his collar mic and the discourse ends.

After a few moments of numbness, we rise slowly and troop out from the mini hall.

The night is poignantly beautiful and very starkly lonely. I am very conscious of the isolation, even as we all head back together on the path. But there is also a sense of strength arising from the knowledge of courage and strength of conviction. The Hindi discourse is not yet over. Guruji's face on the large screen in the meditation hall is clearly visible. We stand outside the hall vacantly, waiting for it to finish. I wonder whether the English language enjoys more brevity of expression than my mother tongue. I am glad I chose the English discourse.

The last meditation session for the day is short. There is just about half an hour left for nine o'clock, when we retire to our rooms and the day at the ashram ends. We head back gratefully. I recoil once again at the sight of the huge grasshoppers. After carefully scanning the door, I dart inside. It is frighteningly lonely in my little room. But there is also no stress of the outside world and no need to rush through anything. I muse at how difficult we make our lives through material possessions and unnecessary rushing to attain meaningless goals.

I decide to put up the mosquito net tonight. I discover, however, that it does not extend till the fourth hook in the wall. I gripe silently at this, but look around for a solution. Maybe I can use the long strap of my denim sling bag, but it falls short. I take down the clothes hangers. Though extremely tired, I attach them together to form an interlinked chain with the strap and it just about extends to the hook on the wall. I am pleased with my effort and ingenuity.

The mosquito net feels claustrophobic. The room is too warm and humid and I am unable to sleep. Familiar demons also raise their heads. I am almost glad for a chance to confront them, as they will not be exorcised until I do. And there is probably no better place where I can do so. I willingly taste the pain. Its magnitude is undiminished.

There are gnawing hunger pangs in my belly. I have not had anything after the puffed rice at five pm. I toss and turn in my bed, plagued with hunger and with worry about the future. I do not know when I finally fall asleep.

3

The Threshold of Pain

❧⟡❧

Day Two

𝒥 AM NOT GROGGY WHEN I WAKE UP. TODAY, I DON THE T-shirt with the long sleeves. Unfortunately, I have no long pants to protect my calves. The sevika starts banging on my door as I am getting dressed. I shout that I am awake, but do not open it. It is still fifteen minutes before time. Gloom starts building inside when I head out into the darkness towards the hall. Guruji has said that the second and sixth days are the hardest and I dread the pain.

I place my water bottle in the little foyer which leads into the hall. The American carries a large steel water bottle and I have started recognizing its sound when she places it in the foyer. The absence of speech has honed our sense of hearing.

We are now required to feel the touch of breaths in our nasal passages. Most of the time, I can only focus on the inflow and outflow of breath and the weak scratchy sensations on my nose. I am hungry and my thoughts are of breakfast and hot tea.

My face feels stretched. The intense concentration has contracted my facial muscles so that my face feels set at an unnatural angle. There is debilitating pain in my legs. It feels like I have not had a moment's rest. I keep shifting in order to disburse the pain, but it does not work. When the two hours of morning meditation are up, I almost crawl to the dining room.

I avoid second helpings. I sip my tea slowly, lost in reverie, though my mind is absorbing all sensory stimuli from my surroundings. As I head towards the washing area, the sevika accosts me and tells me in a low, conspiring tone that she has had a word with the women who wear bangles, but they have told her they cannot take them off. I do not understand and just nod blankly. I seem to be becoming a bit of a zombie here with all the silence.

The sight of the pagoda, ethereally beautiful and pristine white in the morning sunlight, stops me in my tracks as I walk towards my room. I am on the walkway bordering the triangle and it is leafy overhead. It is still a symbol of eternity and infinity. After a few minutes of gazing, I continue walking towards my room.

I decide I will bathe at this hour, as the sevika has suggested. I undress hastily, as if time is short, even though I have an hour. Perhaps I just do not want to think about loneliness or pain and would rather lose myself in action. I touch my belly just before I step in to the toilet. My belly button ring has been bothering me during meditation. I unscrew it. Even after so many years, the sight and feel of it makes me feel wanton and I am better off without it.

I shiver at the touch of cold water on my skin and pour the water slowly over my limbs first to get over the shock and sting of it. There is a small wiper in the bathroom and it proves to be inadequate to dry it. I leave wet footprints on the floor of the room. Once dressed, I step back inside the bathroom to check my appearance and notice two prominent lines on my face that were not there till yesterday. There is one on my chin and one in the centre of my forehead. I am horrified at how the hardship of two days has manifested itself. Then, in a sanguine manner, I reason that something so powerful, therapeutic and healing would necessarily have physical and emotional consequences. I move away from the mirror. I will have time aplenty to deal with furrows on my body after I get rid of the furrows in my mind.

A little shock is in store for me. As I step out of the bathroom, I am accosted by the sight of another fat lizard in my room. I almost reel at the sight. Self-pity starts welling inside, but I gather myself. There is a broom outside my room, longer than the icky toilet brush; a more respectable implement with which to oust unwanted guests. As I brandish it near the lizard, it darts around haphazardly and then slips under my bed. The horror of the creature under my bed spurs me into decisive action. Kneeling down, I place the broom gently over it. Ensnared in the soft thistles, it cannot escape and I sweep it right out of the room. A woman is standing in the courtyard and she looks on amazed as the lizard lands close to her. In a split second, a crow perched nearby swoops down and grabs the stunned lizard in its beak.

I am left stunned too. I feel terrible about the lizard meeting its end in this horrific manner. The precept about not harming living things has been violated. The vision leaves me with disgust, horror and sadness and I cannot shake it off. Events that would have caused little or no reaction in the outside world are much more poignant and piercing here because life is so much more sacred and living is so much more benign.

I lock my room and step out. My eyes fall on the notice board. I am shocked to learn that the morning session is for three continuous hours. Even more shocking is the knowledge that the next period in the afternoon is from one to five. Along with the other periods of meditation, this adds up to ten and a half hours of meditation every day. Suddenly, the day seems even harder than before.

I am filled with apprehension and fatigue even before I sit

down. I do not immediately get into cross-legged position. There are three hours of meditation ahead. I stretch out my legs. My body is already trembling. I look around the hall as we wait for everyone to come in. It is an octagonal structure. The Buddha's path of enlightenment is an eight-fold one called *Dhamma*. I wonder if the pagoda also has eight spires. As I turn my head to look towards the bottom of the hall, I see a big clock and feel a great sense of joy and relief. I have had no way of knowing the time here in the hall and it has been frustrating. The clock will prove to be both a boon and a curse.

As I look towards the male meditators, I see two of them seated on cushions with wooden backrests. I wonder why these two have been granted this special allowance and whether it may not be taking away from the challenge to endure pain. There is a bigger surprise. The elderly sevika, the third of the trio introduced to us on the first day, is sitting on a chair.

My self-awareness has reached a new level. Each thought that enters my mind now is noted clearly and I do not dwell on pain and anguish during meditation. The pain, however, is maddening. Besides the excruciating pain in my legs, a huge twisted cord of pain has also appeared on the right side of my back. I have to work doubly hard to distract my mind from the agony. I wonder if the others are also going through a similar ordeal. Every time I open my eyes, the American has a serene expression on her face and is in the same lotus position.

The American and I never glance at each other. We stand apart, lost in our own thoughts; though I suspect we are having our own extra-sensory conversations through the medium of the universe.

The break is too short to even remotely assuage the pain in my legs or back. Some meditators linger outside even after the hand bell has been rung. As soon as I sit down, my legs revolt and tremble violently. Just when I feel I cannot handle the immense pain anymore, the male teacher announces group checking of the students. I open my eyes and glance at the clock; only about thirty minutes have gone by since we came back into the hall. I do not know if this means we can stop meditating, but no-one moves and so I continue sitting. Names are being called out. The female teacher's voice is loud and raspy. Four names are called out together. My ears strain to hear my name, but I am not in the first group. I resume meditating.

I feel a nudge. The sevika is telling me to go up to the teacher. I must have been deeper in meditation than I realized. I walk up to the platform with three other women. One of them is N. Four cushions lie at the teacher's feet and we sit down on them. The female teacher enquires from each of us in turn how our meditation is progressing. I reply that it is progressing well. I know my thoughts have narrowed from a very wide spectrum to a much smaller one. My thoughts are also less tormented.

The others apparently do not feel the same and reply that they cannot concentrate. The teacher explains that it is natural for our thoughts to stray. Then she asks if we are observing the vow of silence faithfully and all of us nod our heads, even though I know the others are not adhering as faithfully to it. The teacher tells us to meditate in front of her. We all close our eyes. After only a couple of minutes, she tells us we can go back to our places.

The young sevika always sits on the teacher's side like a favourite disciple. She is looking on interestedly and animatedly. I feel irritation rising. I have had enough of her conversation and her knocking on my door. As we are moving away, I impulsively sidle up to her and tell her softly that I am following all rules here and I would like her to leave me alone. She looks as if she has been shot. Then, she bows her head and folds her hands. Suddenly, I am ashamed of my impulsive action, but since I cannot undo it, I walk back to my seat.

After the group checking, the male teacher announces that we can go to our rooms to meditate or continue in the meditation hall. He also announces that the old students can go to the pagoda. Surprised and envious, I wonder why we have not been allowed to do so.

Wearily, I get up to go to my room, promising myself I will not go off to sleep. The sevika avoids looking into my eyes as I pass her. I am regretful for having caused a sprightly young thing any measure of sadness.

My room is cool and quiet. I cannot risk falling asleep. I decide to meditate sitting on the plastic chair. After all, there are meditators who sit on chairs and with backrests. I am sure it is not a very big violation. The clock is in front of me, across the courtyard. There is an hour and a half of meditation to be done. It is a morbid prospect. It is a little too draughty for my liking with a strong breeze blowing in, so I face the chair away from the door and put my aching legs up on the bed. I feel a blessed sense of relief and start focusing on sensations inside my nasal passages. There is a lot of noise outside the room. Women are hanging out washing, sweeping their rooms, opening or closing their doors noisily and even talking! I feel a mixture of anger and derision.

Stray thoughts that come into my mind now sometimes hang incomplete like motes in the air and either vanish instantly or fade away without developing into full-blown visuals. Their stopping at that nascent stage is wondrous and makes me believe I am making progress upon the path.

The thoughts may have become infrequent, but there is nothing that can be done about drowsiness. In spite of my best efforts, I start to fall into a dreamless stupor after every couple of minutes. Sheer will power makes me rouse myself as soon as I become aware of my swaying body, but sleep seems to be winning the battle. I spend about an hour doing nothing more than attempting to keep awake, but then I am jolted into the realization of wasted time and I straighten myself up in the chair, put my legs down on the floor and start to concentrate with renewed will.

The bell rings softly for lunch. Relief washes over me. I make my way in a trance-like state to the dining hall. The sevika dutifully averts her eyes even while she ladles out the food into my plate. I have barely started eating when a female meditator appears at my shoulder and points to a small number painted on to the table where I am seated. She says where I am sitting is her designated place. With a rush of embarrassment, I realize that everyone has been seated all this while according to the numbers corresponding to the room numbers. At the same time, I am vexed that this should matter considering there really is not much dearth of place here. Without any argument, I stand and move off to find my designated place. But the matter is not finished. Another woman is sitting on my seat and now I have to break my silence and explain the situation to her. I quietly point to the number on her table and then point to myself, hoping she will understand the pantomime. Fortunately, she does and moves off, leaving me to finally eat my lunch in peace.

The sun is overhead when I emerge from the dining hall, but it is not very strong. I muse that August is not as fierce this year. May be it is the cool, green environs that are responsible or maybe it is an illusion of coolness caused by the stillness of our bodies.

Since I have already bathed, I lie down gratefully on my bed. I am asleep in seconds. My body clock and the heightened awareness of time do not, however, let me sleep for long. After only about forty minutes, much to my chagrin and disgust, I am awake. The familiar pain rises in my soul and I wonder when succour will come.

I wait for the bell to ring with my eyes closed. But unable to rest, I rise from the bed to refresh myself. I observe the lines on my chin and forehead again. However hard we try to keep away the testimonials to our trials and tribulations in life, they always manifest themselves in the end.

There are fifteen minutes left for the afternoon session to begin. The walkway is cool and I stroll there, subconsciously examining the foliage. Today, the Italian and the American are also strolling outside. All of us wander slowly around the walkway till the bell rings and then we proceed slowly and apprehensively towards the hall. The horrible chord of pain in my back has already reared its head in glee at the thought of overpowering me. As for my poor legs, they have not got any hiatus to recover from their constant punishing ordeal.

I have developed a pattern of pose-changing during meditation. It has evolved out of the dire need to withstand the pain. I do not stay in the cross-legged pose for any length of time. The effort required for mental concentration and to bear the overwhelming pain is causing untold mental and physical agony. The pain in my back does not abate when I shift. It is like a tremendous weight bearing down on me. My legs feel as if they are going to explode. I long to lie down.

After about an hour, the audio tape is switched on and Guruji tells us to try and observe the nostrils used for inhalation and exhalation. *This whole nose thing is really getting too much*, I complain silently, in the throes of agony. And do we not breathe through both nostrils at the same time? What exactly is Guruji trying to make us achieve?

As I try to find out if we really inhale and exhale through different nostrils, I also muse that there is very little emotional upheaval inside me now. It has largely been replaced by a deep awareness of the self. I am on a solitary journey in my own universe. No one and nothing else matters anymore.

I am moving more frequently now, following the same pattern, but no amount of shifting is lessening the terrible pain. My mind also seems to be getting habituated to this pattern. I now determine, out of sheer frustration, to not move at all. I get back into the cross-legged pose.

Instantly, my legs feel as if they are inflamed to twice their size. I remain immobile, focusing intently on my nose and my breathing. The pain rises to a previously unknown crescendo. I am at a threshold of pain which I have not previously experienced. Still I remain motionless; hanging onto the knowledge that moving will not bring me relief for more than a few seconds. It is as if I am suspended in time, torn apart by waves of pain which lash furiously at my body.

Suddenly, the pain in my legs abates on its own, as if the waves have receded a little into the sea. The pain is suddenly bearable even though it has not disappeared. I am filled with wonder at having crossed a huge threshold of pain. It is the first miracle that I experience here. I carry on sitting in the cross-legged pose, riding the gentler waves of pain. When I finally move, it is not out of desperation.

My heart fills with gladness. There is also a new discovery. I think I can now feel the breath entering my nostrils. The nasal septum has suddenly announced its existence and I am conscious of its bend inside my nose.

In the break after two hours of meditation, I exit the hall with a deep sense of accomplishment. As I stand and muse over the incident in the hall, the girl who had entered the ashram in high heels walks past. She is looking very different from the smart, snazzy girl who had walked in confidently that day. She is dressed tackily and her frizzy black hair is tied up. She is also wearing spectacles. Since I don't stare at anyone and my eyes are usually downcast when I am in close vicinity of another meditator, I end up staring at her feet. She is wearing bright orange nail paint on her toenails.

I consider my own appearance. I am dressed very simply and my hair is tied up. Much later, after I return from the ashram, a male friend will ask me teasingly if I distracted all the meditators at the ashram and I will reply that I was just another *sadhika*; but I cannot not be aware that I attract quite a bit of curiosity.

A few years back, I became conscious of the fact that I have uneven features. It brought me a little measure of sadness. Whenever someone calls me beautiful, I think of my small eyes and my bent nose which also boasts of a huge red birthmark on its left side. My eyes are tilted at slightly different angles, too, which give them either a slightly squinty or lost look. I remember wishing I had even features. It was a wistful phase of longing that lasted a couple of months. Perhaps it was just to do with eroded self-esteem, even while everyone around me gushed over my prettiness.

Back in the meditation hall, the pain in my back is unbearable. I do not test myself on crossing the threshold of pain now. I have done it once and I am satisfied that I can control the pain beyond tolerance levels if I so wish. I am terribly glad when it's time for tea.

We are each handed out a banana at tea time and I decide to save it. I am conscious of the fact that I may be breaking rules. Every action and thought is greatly magnified here, with our exposure to the outside world being suddenly so limited. I wrap it up quickly in my handkerchief and make my way out of the dining hall as innocently as I can. I feel like a criminal but take solace in the fact that hunger will just lead to distraction and an inability to meditate properly. Surely a small banana would not be a gross violation.

I am alone as I head back towards the residential blocks. I am glad there is no one around to discover my petty thievery. I walk back as quickly as I can to my room, even though quick has taken on an altogether different meaning now. I am sure I can walk fast if I truly want to, but it will have to be an effort of will, since my body has acquired a silence and stillness that is hard to shake off. I place my banana on the stone slab in the room, atop a little jar of cotton swabs, to keep it away from ants. *Tonight I shall not remain awake because of hunger.*

There is not much time until six, the next hour of meditation. As I wash and moisturize my face, my eyes fall on the two strips of tablets placed on the slab: my antihistamines and my pain killers, both of which I could not do without on a daily basis before I came here. I have not had to take any of them ever since I stepped into the ashram. I attribute it to lack of stress here. My allergy has not acted up at all and my left shoulder, always contracted in chronic pain, is relaxed. In fact, even though my back hurts terribly during meditation, my shoulder has been left unscathed by the torture. I do not yet know the real reason for this absence of illness and pain.

There is heaviness and cramping in my lower back and belly and I realize with a sinking feeling that I am probably close to my menstrual period. I am relieved that I have come prepared for it, but wonder how I will meditate with the additional pain and discomfort.

I have begun believing I am premenopausal. I am nearly thirty-eight; not an age where I would expect to be thinking about menopause, but I had noticed many changes in the preceding months. I sought my doctor friend's advice and he revealed that I may be premenopausal. It was startling and disturbing for me. It seems unimportant now, but the idea of bodily atrophy made me sad then.

I don't know why it is that in spite of knowing the realities of life, we find it so difficult to accept the inevitable.

The evening is approaching, though it is still broad daylight. Peacocks are calling rather frantically, now that they are about to retire for the evening. I walk pensively towards the meditation hall, feeling cramped and heavy and dreading pain. The Italian and the American are about, too, looking as pensive, thoughtful and lost. I wonder what thoughts are going on through their minds. I see the old lady with the gold nose studs often looking tired and strained, as if the process of giving up her demons is taking a big toll on her.

I am now able to feel the touch of breath inside my nasal passages. It is warm and wet and seems to kindle the parts that it touches on its way down into the windpipe. The sharp pricks feel like little advancing arrows as the breath makes its way in. My entire nose is inflamed from within, as if I have the flu. The sensations are now focused more towards the inside than the outer region of the nose and I am amazed at the progress that has been made.

We seven soul sisters walk slowly towards the meditation hall, glad to be able to savour the beauty of the outdoors in the cool air of the evening. The peacocks are calling out goodnight rather forlornly. We all seem to loathe going inside the hall. Surprisingly, it is locked. It seems like our little minority has been forgotten. I am not complaining, but am a little worried about not being back in the meditation hall on time.

Finally, the door is unlocked from inside. It is almost dark. We troop inside quietly and take our places on the cushions. I observe the American, the girl with the orange nail polish, the old lady with the gold nose studs, N and a cherub-faced plump girl with short hair. In this close proximity, it is natural to look at each other though a frank, free appraisal is obviously missing and we do not make eye contact. The bespectacled man walks in and sits on the other side. The discourse of the second day begins.

The cherubic and smiling face of Guruji comes on. He is wearing a crisp white shirt with a green wraparound, which I presume is a dhoti. His wife is missing from view, though there is a shadow of a human form on his side. Guruji smiles in a benign, knowing fashion and says that though the second day is over, there are still many trials ahead because our minds are infirm. He likens our minds to monkeys, swinging incessantly from one branch to another. Our minds, he says, have the strength of wild animals, capable of wreaking great havoc when uncontrolled. No one can harm us more than our own wild mind. I agree because I have experienced the frenzied madness that comes with uncontrolled thoughts. Guruji says wise men can tame their minds to harness the strength within but asks with a faint smile if we think it is possible to achieve this feat within a day or two. Not really expecting a response, he replies to this himself with an emphatic 'oh no'. This evokes weak giggles. I smile.

Once, Guruji continues, a man questioned the Buddha why he, the all-compassionate one, did not use his powers to instantly liberate each and every being who came to him to attain salvation. With his typical manner of counter-questioning, the Buddha asked the man where he was from. The man replied he was from a place far away. Buddha asked him if he visited his home often and the man replied that he did. The Buddha asked if he knew his way back home and asked if he could give the directions to his friends. When the man replied that he did and could, the Buddha asked if his friends could reach there if they knew the directions but did not walk on those roads themselves. The man replied that that was not possible; they would have to walk on the roads themselves. The Buddha smiled and said it was the same for the path of Dhamma. One could be told the path, but would have to walk on it oneself to attain salvation.

Guruji says in order to quench our thirst, it is we who have to drink water. No one can quench our thirst for us. We can be shown the way, but we have to work out our own salvation without expecting supernatural help. The significance of what Guruji says does not register in my mind, and I will expect miracles and be disappointed and disillusioned when I do not seem to be reaching closer to my goal.

Guruji recites a doha in Pali from ancient times and then explains its meaning. Someone who has become tathāgata, which means that he has reached the final goal of ultimate truth, will only compassionately point out the path. The word seems to hang in the sultry air of the mini hall. I repeat and savour it on my tongue silently. The purpose of my quest here is to seek liberation and become tathāgata. It is a quest for liberation from the shackles of my past.

Guruji says Dhamma, the law of nature, the law of truth or the universal law, which governs both animate and inanimate objects, punishes us if we violate it and rewards us if we live in accordance with it. Once, someone asked Buddha what this universal law was and the Buddha replied that it was no high philosophy. It was also not the monopoly of any one person, as there could be and had been, many Buddhas. Guruji says if we hoped to attain complete liberation and become a Buddha in ten days, though, it was not going to happen. There are some laughs. I do not laugh. I do not expect to become Buddha in ten days, though I do expect a fair amount of liberation.

The teaching of Dhamma, Guruji says, is to abstain from all sinful, unwholesome actions, get ordained in piety and keep purifying the mind. This, he says, is the beauty and totality of Dhamma. It is *pari punnam*, or complete. Unwholesome actions, he says, are physical or vocal actions which harm or hurt other beings and disturb their peace and harmony, whereas wholesome actions are those which support or help other beings to live a harmonious and peaceful life. I can't help thinking of many of my unwholesome actions. Guruji says we experience the truth of wholesome and unwholesome actions as we advance in Dhamma. The first step in Dhamma is to live a life of *sīla* or morality. The second is *samādhi* or concentration and the third is *paññā*, wisdom or insight.

Guruji says everyone understands sīla, but only at an intellectual level. We all know we must not steal or lie or perform any moral outrage. But as we progress along the path, we start experiencing that whenever we perform an unwholesome action, it generates negative energy. Nature, he says, does not want unwholesome actions and the punishment is swift and in the realm of the present, not in the after life.

He says we should give importance to things inside rather than outside and that these ten days of meditation would help us experience the benefit of this for ourselves. It would be akin to putting one's hand in fire and learning that fire burns. It's not a great analogy, but the import is clear. Negative mental volition leads to pain.

The camera zooms in closer to Guruji and I can see the dark circles under his puffy eyes. The consciousness of right and wrong will assume mammoth proportions when I leave the ashram. I will be stretched to breaking point trying to live by the rules of Dhamma, consciously banishing every single negative thought from my mind and only performing those actions, which I consciously decide are wholesome. Even the realm of fantasy while making love will be considered unwholesome by me.

Guruji now explains the eight-fold noble path. Sīla, he says, consists of *Samma Vacha*, *Samma Kamanta* and *Samma Ajiva*: right speech, right action and right livelihood. Right speech meant not telling lies, not using harsh words or indulging in meaningless conversations which wasted time. Right action meant performing wholesome actions and avoiding unwholesome ones. Right livelihood meant working honestly without harming others. If one's livelihood encouraged others to violate their sīla, it would not be right livelihood. He gives the example of an arms dealer, indirectly encouraging killing. He also gives the example of a person rearing animals meant for slaughter. It sounds a little extreme and I wonder if there is any profession which may be regarded as noble in the eyes of Dhamma.

Guruji also says that if the motivation behind one's profession was not noble, the livelihood could be considered noble. He gives the example of a doctor who is upset at fewer number of patients due to fewer epidemics in a particular season. Guruji does not condemn the doctor and says smilingly that business men are far worse. He should know, he says, since he comes from a business background which encouraged profiteering.

Guruji has a very simple and colloquial manner of speaking and his stories, analogies and parables are childlike. Yet, my respect for him is growing each day. I again wonder what made an affluent person like him break from the fold to sit here in his dhoti with a perspiring forehead and preach the benefits of Dhamma to multitudes for nothing in return.

Samma Ajiva does not involve me, I muse. I am a homemaker without any immediate future prospects of a profession. My mind is now drifting. Guruji's concepts of Dhamma have been a little tedious. Now he is talking about the next step of Dhamma: samadhi or mastery of the mind – learning to concentrate the mind with a base of wholesomeness.

Samadhi, he says, consists of *Samma Vayano, Samma Sati and Samma Samadhi*. Samma Vayano means right effort or exercise to control the mind; the kind we have been attempting in the past two days. Guruji says the exercises to control the mind help to get rid of all the voices inside our minds that mislead and misguide us, help to close the doors to mental defilements, preserve existing virtues without letting them be tainted with ego or pride and allow new virtues to enter one's mind.

Samma Sati, he says, is the right kind of awareness: an awareness of the reality of the present, rather than that of the past. Guruji explains that sati, which means memory, cannot include awareness of the past, or of the future, but only of the reality which manifest itself in the present. He says the meditation technique we have been practising – that of observing our breaths from second to second without letting our minds drift between the two undesirable realms of past and future – has increased our faculty of observing the subtlest of sensations. This kind of awareness is *Yatha Botha* or 'as it is', since, on the path of Dhamma, nothing is to be imagined; only experienced. Either tonight or the following day, we would experience subtler sensations, with the area of concentration becoming smaller. We would also feel many physiological changes in our bodies. Finally, we would experience a constant flux or flow in our entire field of matter. He says that we must keep observing the reality which manifests itself and understand that no sensation is eternal, as everything arises and then passes.

Guruji then explains Samma Samadhi, which means concentration without ignorance. He says there should be no confusion or imagination involved in the process of observing reality and the object of concentration should be real. Here, he delves into some of the 'realities' that may be manifested within the body at any given time: sensations of expansion or contraction, heat or cold, dryness or moistness, heaviness or lightness, throbbing and perspiration. Concentration, he says, should be free of craving or aversion.

He tells us we will enter the field of paññā day after tomorrow; the last step in the technique, which takes one to the depth of the mind and thus purifies the very source of all our misery. He then smiles benignly and recites 'bhavatu sabba managalam' thrice, signalling the end of today's discourse. The camera zooms out to reveal his wife, who has been sitting silently and complacently by his side for the last hour and a half.

We walk back slowly lost in thoughts of self-doubt and self-discovery. I can hear the Hindi discourse going on in the meditation hall and I see the big screen with Guruji's face. The humour and colloquialism of the English discourse seem to be missing from the Hindi one.

The women soon pour out of the hall. We never see any of the male meditators, since they have a separate entrance to the meditation hall, separate residential blocks somewhere behind the pagoda and a separate dining area.

We meditate only briefly in the hall and then head to our rooms. In the room, I eat my dinner of the one meager banana with relish, happy that no ants or insects have got to it. I feel happy and satiated. I slip into the net and lie flat on my back, willing myself to relax so that I can get rid of the pain in my back. As I do so, I let myself float in the realm of the past.

The memories still hurt as much as they did before I came here, except that I feel secure and protected here; cut-off from a world I do not want to face right now. No one can reach me here. This is my sanctuary and it is also giving me the strength to fortify myself against future onslaughts. I let myself question my life and its events and allow myself to berate my failings.

My thoughts feel crystal clear. I wonder at the amazing phenomena we are experiencing here with our bodies and the fact that we cannot pick out existing sensations on our body without first training our minds. It excites me that I will be able to share these amazing facts with others once I am out. I wish I could write it all down. Even the most mundane seems important and magnificent. I have a good feeling tonight; I am progressing surely and quickly on the path of liberation and I am ready to write a fantastic book about the quest. I test my nose every couple of minutes to feel renewed wonderment at my capabilities. It flares up obligingly.

The banana has caused a bit of indigestion. There is also a chill in the air. I take my sheet up to my chin, but it does not help much. Sheer weariness keeps me from getting up to take the blanket. My pillow also seems too thin tonight and I fold it over itself to try and create a comfortable headrest.

Deep sleep eludes me. I wake up uneasy and fearful around three in the morning. It is raining heavily outside. My spirits sag. I have not carried an umbrella with me even though it was advised in the guidelines for the course. I do not know how I will make it to the meditation hall in the rain at half past four. I slump back dejectedly into my bed. I am even colder now because of the rain and I finally muster up the strength to get up and switch the fan off and take the moldy and worn blanket upon me. The rain makes a terrific din outside, but I finally fall off to sleep.

4

SKIN AND BONES

✦⁓⁓✦

Day Three

O WAKE UP TO A SENSE OF RELIEF THAT IT IS NOT RAINING anymore. I think I must have said a silent prayer to God just then, but I am not sure, since I have not remembered God much in the past three days. I am aware that my experience here will clash with my religious beliefs and blind faith and I wait for it to happen: ready to accept whatever truth is revealed to me and ready to let go of dogmas.

This morning feels different from the past two days. The air is heavy and soporific. The place feels closed, cloistered and ominous. The walkway is wet. My spirits are low. I do not have my usual early morning energy and enthusiasm. May be the rigours of the past two and a half days have taken their toll. I do not want to enter the meditation hall and sit motionless for two hours, enduring pain and doing the same monotonous task.

At breakfast after morning meditation, I receive the full blast of the cooler in the dining hall. I forsake the milk for a cup of tea. I need to keep awake for the long hours of meditation ahead. I narrate my unwritten book to myself and think of the masterpiece it might become. While going towards the washing area, I ask the sevika, who is behind the food counter, for an umbrella. I am terrified of getting wet in case it rains again. She nods and I heave a sigh of relief.

Outside the dining hall is a small table with a little notepad and pen. A notice above says the meditators can request for items to be bought from the market. Over the course of the next few days, I will see a lot of strange and seemingly unnecessary items listed here and will be shaking my head with amazement.

My brain feels feverish. It is becoming harder and harder to chronicle everything in my mind, especially since there is no spectacular change in our everyday routine. I fear I will be unable to remember it all eight days later. I again have the urge to write down everything that has happened so far. It would lessen the pressure in my mind and free it to focus only on meditation. I head for my room faster than I have in days with an obsessive urgency. I do not have any pen and paper, but I have something else which will do for now: a roll of toilet paper and my black kohl pencil. I am aware I am acting like a woman possessed, but I am also convinced I need to do this to preserve all the sensory inputs of the last three days.

I place a piece of flimsy toilet paper on the stone slab and start writing furiously. The soft pencil tip threatens to break, so I reduce the pressure of my hand. I am frenzied; there is so much to write about and the chronological sequence is a bit distorted now. I write about peacocks and respiration, meals and meditators. The pencil tip is wearing down fast. I even jot down the bit about my daughter crying while leaving, though I know it is something that will never be erased from my mind.

The tip finally wears down completely. There is still a lot to write, but most of it has been recorded. I wonder what I will do henceforth. There are many days left to go and there will be a lot more which will compete for memory space in my mind. Just then, I remember the writing pad and pen outside the dining hall. Maybe I can take the pen and a few pages from the pad. The pen will surely be replaced. There is not much time left if I want to do so now and I rush in to bathe after carefully concealing the smudgy notes under my blanket on the shelf.

After my bath, I walk slowly towards the dining hall. I have no excuse for heading there at this time and I pretend I am looking for something I have lost as I walk. But there are stragglers still coming out of the dining hall after a leisurely breakfast. My plan is foiled and I turn back dejectedly.

As we wait in the meditation hall, I observe the American closely. Her right leg is out and I spot a tattoo on her right ankle. It is a strange, spidery tattoo and resembles a tree with thin bare boughs. I wonder why one would ever get such a tattoo. But then, I remember my own. It looks like a big blob from a distance, even though at close range, it is a work of art: the face of a leopard entwined with a snake. It has a significant symbolism. When I was about twelve, I read a beautiful book about a she-leopard who is orphaned as a cub and brought up by a cheetah family. Though she loves her foster family, the leopard cannot change her true nature and ultimately returned to her kind. Hers is a solitary quest much as mine has been. Her traits match mine – dignity, courage and honour. Felines have always fascinated and attracted me and if I were an animal, I would definitely be a feline.

The familiar, terrible pain is back. Thankfully, at around half past nine, the male teacher announces that there will be group checking. When my group is called up, the female teacher asks gently once again how we are progressing. N says in a quivering voice that she just cannot manage to sit in the meditation hall anymore. The teacher calmly tells her she will get used to it. N further says she lost her temper with the sevika this morning. I look at her in surprise. I wonder what has transpired; I did not hear or see anything. The teacher tells her it is alright. Unlike me, N does not seem contrite after having complained about the sevika. She looks as if she is about to gripe a lot more, but the teacher moves on to the next girl who says she gets very agitated during meditation when she thinks about her relatives. This does not make much sense to me, but perhaps it is a big issue in a joint family in our country, with the aspirations of young people sometimes heavily curbed.

The third girl asks if it is necessary to go into the rooms to meditate when we are allowed to do so and the female teacher says it is up to us, if we wish a break from the monotony and the discomfort of the hall. I feel relieved hearing this, as if my sitting in the chair or on the bed has just been sanctioned.

I now ask the teacher if we can go into the pagoda to meditate. The teacher looks quite surprised and says that we can do so from the fifth day onwards. I am disappointed and want to ask the reason for the wait, but refrain. I do not want to reveal my fascination with the pagoda lest it seem strange, but an explanation seems appropriate, so I tell her I asked because it is always far too noisy in the residential block. I expect her to question why, but she doesn't.

It is ten o'clock. We are given permission to go to our rooms. I know now that it is futile for me to try and meditate for one full hour in my room. I decide I will sleep for half an hour and then try and meditate for the remaining time. It turns out I am not successful in doing either.

Before leaving my room, I sling my denim bag across my chest. I may have an opportunity to steal some paper. I linger for a few seconds outside the dining hall after lunch to see if I can pilfer a couple of pages and the pen, but there are too many people around. The sevika is also present and since I know I will be getting my period soon, I ask her for some newspaper to wrap the waste, but she proclaims with a fervent shaking of her head that we are not allowed newspapers here. I explain softly why I require it and she then reluctantly agrees to get me some, though she still looks a little unconvinced.

As I walk back, I think of the teachers in the meditation hall, writing notes from time to time. I have wondered what they write and suspected nervously that it is something of a progress report of the students. The paper and pens may be lying in the meditation hall. I walk towards it. As it is rather strange to be around the hall at this time of day, I once again search the ground intently as I have lost something. At the entrance, I quickly open the door and head inside. Two clipboards with loose sheets and pens are placed on tables next to the teachers' chairs. My eyeballs pop with excitement and with fear. Someone may come in, especially from the male entrance. But there is no time to be lost and the urge is too great. I race to the platform and hurriedly pull off a few sheets of paper and grab a pen. I drop them into my sling bag and rush outside with a palpitating heart.

I finally have my coveted writing equipment! When I reach my room, I start scribbling furiously. I even copy out the notes I had written on the toilet paper. Surprisingly, though, the writing does not lessen the strain on my mind. If anything, the silent narrative is stronger than before and I feel almost nauseous. It is almost half past twelve. I decide to wash my hair in order to avoid thinking too much.

I feel a little better after I am done. I do not have enough time to dry and comb them and realize it will be four hours before I can do so. I hurriedly run my fingers through it. I feel different with my hair open – more feminine and human, and definitely cooler in the afternoon heat.

I feel fearful as I re-enter the scene of crime. Will the missing pen create a furore? No one here takes anything belonging to another, so I fervently hope it will be assumed that it has rolled off or something. I fancy that my guilt is visible on my face. Thoughts of being found out or questioned plague me. Like an extremely conscientious meditator, I hurry to my place and close my eyes because I do not want to have to look at the female teacher when she comes in. The male teacher is already in. When I peek through half-closed eyes, I see he has picked up the clipboard. I am panicking inside. I will myself to forget what has happened, telling myself it was necessary.

The afternoon session, as always, is the most gruesome. There is enormous pain all over. It has extended from my back to my neck. Every day, newer parts of my body are being engulfed. The only silver lining seems to be that I am obtaining more fodder for my book.

My hair is still wet and a few strands blow on to my face with the breeze of the fan. This makes my nose ticklish but provides a wonderful plethora of sensations to focus on. I quite forget Guruji's advice about focusing on the feeblest sensations.

A little chord of pain has appeared on the right side of my forehead, extending from the hairline to the temple. It is akin to the chord of pain in my back; only smaller in size. My head feels as if it is going to explode. I know most of the strain is due to the immense burden my book is putting on me and the wrongdoing I have committed by stealing the pen and paper. I have broken an important precept of the ashram. I have violated my sīla. The fact that I have done it for a good cause and that I will return the pen eventually is no solace.

Around three o'clock, I realize N is not on her place in front of me. I suspect she is unwell, but I disapprove of the laxity.

I finally dare to look up at the stage in the break. The female teacher is looking unperturbed and I am very relieved, though I wonder if it is because she has had no use for the pen till now or its disappearance does not matter much. The American has walked up to the male teacher. We have been allowed to go up to the teachers in the breaks to ask questions. The American has gone up a few times, but always to the male teacher. I envy her as I find it difficult to express myself in Hindi to the female teacher.

In the break, I use my fingers to untangle my hair and comb it out. The sun feels almost benevolent on my damp head. I half close my eyes in somnolence, but then see the sevika approaching with a long-handled black umbrella. She hands it to me and with relief, I place it carefully next to my bottle in the foyer.

I am calmer after the break. It seems my crime has not been detected, even though the guilt will not go until the following day. The pressure in my head has not reduced though, and it is an awful strain to concentrate. As I am trying to focus on the sensations inside my nose with all my being, I suddenly find myself levitating. Or that is how it feels. I am stunned but exhilarated. Is this another miracle? I remain in that state of seeming weightlessness for many seconds, before I feel the weight of my body upon my cushion once again.

In the dining room at tea time, I slip an apple from my meal tray into my sling bag. I will not eat it at night and risk indigestion and sleeplessness, but have it in the morning before meditation, to stave off the morning hunger pangs. I do not feel so guilty anymore because I have noticed a few old ladies openly taking fruit out of the dining hall.

I walk back quickly to the room, to be able to write about the levitation and the apple. Now that I have the luxury of writing everything in detail, I leave out almost nothing; even the most insignificant incident is noted. I hide the sheets carefully under the blanket lest the inquisitive sevika spots them. I'm glad for it because immediately after, there is a knock on my door and I see her standing there with the newspaper I had requested. I thank her and close the door.

I do not look at the print of the newspaper. It is a Hindi tabloid and has a lot of pictures of film stars in it. I presume it is dated. I place it on the top shelf. I decide to write my notes now in the three breaks after breakfast, lunch and tea so that there is no longer a constant urge to write.

In the evenings, there is always a feeling of wistfulness. I think about what I have lost and what I will gain. There is also a sense of peace, because my body and soul start to unwind a little from the strain of the day and I look forward to the discourse for its visual stimulus, a change from the monotony of meditation. Today, however, I am downcast and weary. It has been emphasized that there should be no reading or writing material on our person here and I know it is for a reason. I am also too wise to not know that it interferes with the process and progress of meditation. I am concentrating more on my book than on the technique. I came here foremost to heal and for strength and succour; the idea of the book just happened because of the experiences here.

The peacocks have started their cacophonic litany once again. The pagoda looks beautiful in the dusk; as beautiful as it does in the early mornings. I stop to gaze at it as I would gaze at a lover's face, admiring even deep lines and furrows. I stop to count the spires atop the structure. There are eight of them.

When it is time for the discourse, I walk with head bent towards the mini hall. Tonight, the pain of the past is more acute and I feel sorry for myself for the first time in three days. Guruji said that the second and sixth day would be the hardest, but for me, today is harder than yesterday. The fortitude inside is rapidly crumbling.

I simply cannot sit in the mini hall during the discourse without a backrest anymore. The pain is far too acute. The American has propped herself against the wall perpendicular to the rows of cushions and I decide to do the same. There are extra cushions near the television set and taking one of these, I take my place next to the American.

There are a lot of insects inside the mini hall. They keep creeping in from under the door and there is a lot of shifting around as the squeamish meditators try and avoid a bug or a frisky frog which has hopped in. The insects and the frogs do not bother me. I frequently brush or throw them away to help out my cringing soul sisters. No words are exchanged, but I can feel the gratitude.

N is not in the mini hall. I start to wonder where she is.

Guruji has a blue chadar wrapped around his waist today. Without any preamble, he announces that tomorrow is the day we will enter the field of paññā. The first three days have been preparatory. We have practised sīla and samadhi for three days, but these cannot take us to the goal of full liberation. Gautama Buddha practised perfect sīla and samadhi as a means of attaining liberation and enlightenment but he could not achieve them till he reached the depths of his mind through paññā. Guruji says that there are sleeping defilements in the depths of the mind which need to be taken out. As he says this, I have a vision of twisted demons being pulled out from my mind, screaming in agony and a new me emerging like my favourite mythical phoenix.

Guruji explains that paññā consists of the right type of thought and right type of understanding. He says when we start observing our minds, we realize how much negativity is there in the form of overpowering thoughts of anger, hatred, sadness, pain and passion, but as we continue observing objectively, these slowly change and become less violent. They are no longer as negative and start pertaining more to the present. My eyes widen with amazement. This has happened with me since I have come here.

Right understanding, he says, may be *sutmaya paññā* or someone else's wisdom which one accepts because of blind faith. I think of my holy book and my dependence on it. It may also be *chintamaya paññā*, which means understanding through intelligence. But *bhavnāmaya paññā;* he says, in a low, admiring tone and a shake of his head as if he can't begin to explain the wonders of it; means to happen, or to live the wisdom; a direct experience of truth.

He explains bhavnāmaya paññā with the simple analogy of a person who goes to a restaurant. The person salivates when he looks at the menu. Then he sees others enjoying their food and this whets his appetite even more because of the presence of the food, which he can observe. But it is only when his own meal is placed before him and he actually eats the food, that he can experience its taste. Looking at the menu is sutmaya paññā; seeing others eat is chintamaya paññā and eating the food is bhavnāmaya paññā.

Bhavnāmaya paññā makes us aware of the impermanence of things. Though we understand the concept of impermanence intellectually, we do not really apply it to our lives. Guruji gives the example of how we feel when someone close to us passes away. For a while, we have a new perspective on the futility of life's longing and desires, but soon after, we are back to our lives of craving. He also explains this in a humorous way. He says people listen to discourses about the futility of attachments to material things, but as soon as they step out of the discourse, they start looking for their footwear and agitating over someone having walked away with them. I smile, a little shamefacedly. Even in this place, where we have no possessions of any value with us and where stealing would be out of the question (even though I have committed a theft just a few hours back), I am bothered about my water bottle and umbrella and always strive to keep them in a secure place. It seems one can never be really free of attachment to things.

Guruji gives example of impermanence: a candle flame and a river. Both are never the same at any given second. The particles of the flame die out constantly and new ones rise, and the water in the river flow on and new water replaces it. But, to our ignorant minds, they are perceived as permanent. The speed of change in everything creates illusion, delusion and confusion that there is solidity, whereas everything is nothing but wavelets. He says it is something we have to experience for ourselves; the fact that the human body is also changing every second. He says there is a long path ahead of us to reach this realization. I do not heed these words, probably because I am thinking about flames and rivers. In the next three days, my impatience to achieve will lead to a huge amount of agitation and depression.

This talk about matter being wavelets or particles in a constant state of vibration or the fact that everything is impermanent is not new. I want the discourse to get over to clear the confusion regarding the book with the teacher. I fear I may go mad if I don't.

Guruji says by dividing, disintegrating, dissolving and dissecting, we are able to reach the ultimate truth and something beyond mind and matter: the tiniest subatomic particle which the Buddha called *kalapa*. It is made up of eight elements which cannot be separated, like earth, water, air and fire. By the time he snaps his fingers or blinks his eyes, he says, these subatomic particles arise and fade trillions of times. A prize-winning scientist from the West, he says a trifle depreciatingly, reached the same conclusion about the subatomic particles that liberated souls did through bhavnāmaya paññā. He adds, though, that we must not belittle the findings of the scientist, as the Nobel Prize is not given to every Tom, Dick and Harry. There is no laughter, but I am sure there must have been a few smiles.

The first truth that we experience through bhavnāmaya paññā, he continues, is the truth of change. What seems at first to be solidified apparent reality, of bones and flesh and solidified sensations in the form of heat, pain and pressure, becomes subtler till the entire structure is nothing but vibrations; a constant flow or flux of energy which reveals the truth of impermanence. It is then that the madness of attachment towards the physical structure starts going away.

The first part of wisdom, Guruji elaborates further, is *anicca* or impermanence. The second is *dukkha*, which means the knowledge of misery; misery which results from both aversions and cravings. A meditator starts with painful, solidified sensations and starts reacting adversely to them, but a stage comes on the seventh, eighth, ninth or tenth day or sometimes not till the next course for some meditators, when a free flow of vibrations starts occurring in the body. The meditator starts craving this free flow. He starts asking the teachers why one meditation session is good and another isn't. I shall be doing precisely the same thing soon enough, not understanding that the entire purpose of the process was to maintain equanimity in the face of both the desirable and the undesirable.

Guruji says *anattā* or the concept of 'I', is illusory, because we are nothing but bubbles. Though, he says smilingly, for the purpose of worldly interactions, we do have to resort to an identity. He says beauty is supposed to be one-sixteenth of an inch deep, but if we take out that much thickness of skin and examine it, we would be hard-pressed to find any beauty. How much we are attracted to the physical body of a man or woman, he exclaims, though a body is nothing but flesh and bones and if it were disintegrated into its parts, there would be no beauty left to see.

All of us know that beauty is misleading, illusory and superficial. But to hear it being described in terms of flesh and bones is a new, disturbing concept. Guruji says a single strand of hair, when taken from its mass of beautiful tresses, is hardly a thing of beauty. It is the same with nails and teeth; if even one was taken out and examined individually, it would be repulsive. Even a man's muscular arms, admired by an enamoured woman, would not be an object of admiration any more if they were disintegrated into sinews. Beauty was just an idea. Disintegrate anything beautiful into its component parts and nothing would be beautiful anymore.

Hot tears sting my eyes. Lest they pour out, I get up from my cushion against the wall and quickly make my way out into the darkness. Leaning against a wall near the dining hall, I cry over the futility of attraction and attachments. I wish little children were told all the ugly stuff about beauty at a very early age. There would be no more broken hearts and torn souls.

I can see the television from the window in front of me. I'm glad no one can see me crying. When I am sufficiently composed, I make my way back in and sit down on my cushion. No one seems to have been disturbed by my hasty exit. Guruji is saying we should not develop hatred towards beauty but should try and achieve a state of pure love and compassion.

Talking about paññā once again, he says if we expect to feel billions of subatomic particles in a state of motion right away, we will be disappointed. He also warns that when we go inside the depths of our bodies and minds, it should not be to quench the thirst of inquisitiveness: another advice that will be unheeded by me. I must have still been thinking of sinews.

We have come to the end of the discourse. Guruji says he wishes all of us real peace, real harmony and real happiness.

I make my way back rather quickly towards the meditation hall. We stand outside the hall, waiting. There are huge grasshoppers around the bulb which is suspended from the aluminium eaves and they are hopping on the ground near the hall steps as well. We all stay beyond the range of their scampers.

As soon as the meditators come out for their break, I move in. Fortunately for me, the female teacher is not in her place. I walk up to the stage and stand in front of the male teacher. I look directly at him, waiting for him to look up. I know instinctively that he is aware I am more comfortable conversing in English and he can probably sense my agitation. He has counselled the American, who has gone up to him a few times and I know he will not turn me away. Still, I am a little nervous. He is a good looking, suave man and I have felt fortified to have someone like him here in a position of authority, even though there is almost no interaction between the teachers and us. I am also very conscious that though we are only supposed to ask questions related to the technique, I am about to ask him something that is very personal to me.

The teacher looks up. He gesticulates briskly and pleasantly for me to sit. I pull a cushion and sit down at his feet. Unfortunately, my voice comes out in a croak. I have rehearsed a bit of what I want to say – an old trick to avoid gaffes – and I am surprised I can barely speak. Tears threaten to pour out. Making my voice firmer, I tell the teacher that the previous two days have been stupendous, at which he smiles approvingly and nods his head. My next sentence, however, changes his countenance.

I inform him I am very disturbed and that it has been a difficult day. I tell him that I am a writer, because this is relevant to what I need to ask him; but I think there is also an element of vanity in the sharing of this fact. He seems impressed; I assume this because he asks me my name and names are altogether unnecessary here. As I tell him my name and hope he does not ask me how many bestsellers I have to my credit, I can't help thinking of a future time when I would be a celebrated writer and he would read a book written by me. He would, of course, receive due mention for mentoring me. Even in my agitated state and in these environs, pride and vanity have not been destroyed. The teacher nods his head and I inform him that there is a huge strain in my mind because I am always recounting things to myself for a book I may be writing about my stay here. I ask him if I can keep doing this and expectedly, he disagrees. He explains that the technique is going to get deeper and richer and I will need all my attention to be focused on it and it alone.

Even though I am not wholly convinced about giving up my precious writing and recounting, I feel relieved, as if a weight has been gently lifted off my shoulders. I long to also tell the teacher about the theft, but fortunately, I am not foolish enough to do so even in such a vulnerable state of mind.

The teacher tells me there will be subsequent courses in the future, so there is no need for me to try and remember each experience in detail and I am surprised at his assumption that I would want to go through this again and angry and upset that he does not understand that my book is supposed to be about this particular first experience. I tell him firmly that there won't be any subsequent courses for me, but thank him for his advice.

The female teacher is back in her place and I wonder if she is annoyed that I have consulted the male teacher. The hall is full and the meditators are waiting for instruction. I go back to my seat, feeling embarrassed. I will now concentrate solely on meditation. But even as I resolve this, I find myself recounting the incident with the teacher as if I am reading a passage from my book.

As I step out of the hall, I am filled with both wonderment and sadness. The night is sonorous with the noise of crickets and brilliant stars twinkle in the sky. I have never looked towards the sky while walking back at night. Tonight, I gaze upwards. Suddenly, I see the light of an aeroplane in its trajectory high up in the sky. Why this should be such a huge, monumental and wondrous sight, I do not know, except maybe being isolated from most sensory inputs so commonplace in the outside world has dramatically altered my perception. Aeroplanes seem alien here.

I stop on the path. Meditators walk past me, but I do not care if I look strange standing there, gaping. I am in my own esoteric world and I already know I am different from everyone else here. I spot two more aeroplanes. I am transfixed. It is like I have suddenly discovered the bridge linking isolation and civilization. I am both ecstatic and crestfallen. Ecstatic because the aeroplanes are a link to the world outside, and crestfallen because that world is full of suffering.

As I walk on, images course through my mind: images of my life outside the ashram and images of my book with its pages coming apart and flying loose in the wind.

On reaching my room, I lie down in bed and feel the ache in every pore of my body. The pain does not recede even with the supine pose. It washes over me in waves: relentless waves of penance. My heart is heavy with a feeling of loss but it has also been enriched with wisdom.

I go over the happenings of the day. I have been through a whole plethora of emotions today, encompassing a wide and extreme spectrum. I wonder if I should throw away my notes. Gradually, I come to the conclusion that it can do no harm to preserve what has already been written. The decision gives me a little peace after all the turbulence I have been through.

I try and taste the old, familiar pain upon my tongue. It is still there, but it is mixed, strangely, with compassion. I can forgive and let go. The knowledge is a revelation and feels like a benediction. I cannot bless those who have harmed me, but I can move on to a place where the sharp stabs of pain will not hurt any more. The feeling of forgiveness and compassion, both towards myself and the ones who have hurt me gives me peace for the first time in months and I eventually sleep with a sad smile on my face, despite the pain.

5

THE 'WHITE LIGHT'

❦

Day Four

$\mathcal{I}$T IS RAINY AND STORMY. I WAKE UP TO A FEELING of gloom inside and outside, but I am glad for my umbrella. I wonder about the meditators who have not catered for the rain, but I am infinitely more bothered about myself. I chew the apple I had stolen yesterday at tea without enjoyment; I doubt it will do anything for the knots in my stomach or assuage any hunger pangs and it doesn't.

It is not very pleasant to walk in the rain in the dark. I place my umbrella on the shoe rack outside; no one uses it to place shoes on. Numerous pairs of shoes lie scattered around.

Today is the day we are supposed to receive the instructions for *vipassanā* or insight, but my thoughts are still centred on the book. I have been advised to give it up, but I cannot seem to let go completely as I fear the memory traces of all sensory information will dissipate over the next few days if not constantly rehearsed.

I open my eyes sometime during the morning session and see the dawn breaking outside. It is a cold, gloomy dawn. I see the sevika gently and silently pulling open the curtains. There are scattered grey clouds in the sky when we emerge from the hall for breakfast. I spy a whole row of umbrellas hanging from a bar outside the hall. It makes my endeavour for preparedness seem futile, as the rest have received without even asking. The only consolation I have is that the black umbrella is ubiquitous now and I do not have to guard mine.

I walk back from the dining hall as if the weight of the world is on my shoulders. I have neat, detailed notes about the first two days here and I am sorely tempted to continue writing. However, the main purpose of my being here is not to create a book, but to heal and I cannot lose sight of the fact. The notes are dead weight pulling me down. Even though I had decided last night to save what was already written, I know I cannot move on until I let go completely. I will only be able to stop concentrating so intensely on the book when I destroy the dead weight.

When I reach the room, I will destroy the notes for which I have toiled and erred.

I cannot dither, for I may change my mind. I quickly pull out the coveted sheets and proceed to tear them up into tiny indecipherable fragments, which I throw into a huge bin placed in one corner of the courtyard. A pigeon atop a redundant water heater in the oppcsite corner watches me quizzically. I feel as if I have killed a part of me and I have an urge to pluck the dumb pigeon from its low, comfortable perch and make it pay for my loss. The dead weight is gone but the furrows will take longer to go. And the pen and the stolen sheets remain tucked away under the blanket: a proof of my sin and inability to resist temptation. These must be returned to their rightful place.

I have to fight the urge to sleep and try and forget everything. But my resolve and determination to proceed on the path of right karma stops me. I bathe, tidy up the room and leave the block. As I turn on to the triangular walkway, I spot a peacock sitting on the lowest branches of a stunted tree in the open grassy area just a few metres away. It is only a couple of feet from the ground and its beautiful tail is almost brushing the earth. It sits motionless and I am mesmerized and reminded of pictures of Vrindavan, the childhood abode of Lord Krishna. This scene seems straight out of images of gods and goddesses in their fantasy worlds of beautiful forests, doting beasts and overflowing pots of sovereigns.

I stand and stare for a long time. It is a beautiful sight and I do not have much else to do. The girl who sits adjacent to me in the hall appears. She has a swinging, carefree walk, as if she is on holiday. She also spots the peacock and seems equally entranced with the sight. She seems to be smiling. I move on, head bent low in thought. The sight of the peacock, now shared with someone else, has lost its charm and symbolism for me. However, the image seems to leap out gleefully from the pages of an unwritten book.

I can smell the sensual fragrance of wet earth. I have been wearing my black flip flops for days and it is glorious unencumbering to be squelching through the wetness. In spite of the terrible pain in my legs and my back, dread for the long hours of meditation and the sorrow for my book, there is a feeling of real peace within.

It is only eight o'clock but it already feels like half the day is gone. In the first break at nine, the sevika walks up to N's place in the hall. It is still empty. She removes the cushion. I am confused and almost about to protest, but she gesticulates for me to move up the row. Dumbfounded, I do as I'm told, so that I am now sitting next to the Italian. The sinking feeling that N is here no more destroys my already fragile courage. We have seven more days to go. I know I will not quit, but how much harder will this get and how much more pain will I have to endure?

I move out in a state of numbness. The events of yesterday and the thought of N having left are almost too much to handle. Fortunately, I do not yet know what lies ahead, or I would have followed in N's footsteps just then.

The sun is out and it feels warm upon my shoulders and arms. It is a strange thing to like the sun in the month of August in India, but I am at a strange threshold in my life, too. I feel cleansed, though my mind is in disarray. I think about N and wonder if I will ever meet her again. I do not even know her last name.

I can look at the female teacher now without too much fear or guilt. I try to see if the missing pen has been replaced or if she seems perturbed by its absence, but I cannot make out either. She is too far away, even though I have moved up in the row and am now closer to the platform. I have already absolved myself of my sin with my resolve to return the pen, and the talk with the male teacher has been a sort of absolution as well.

Battling the ever-agonizing pain, I go back to meditating, but my attention is constantly diverted from my nose to my forehead, where the chord of pain throbs dangerously. Except for my left shoulder, my whole body is a mass of agony.

After lunch, I hurry out because I need to go back into the meditation hall to return the pen. I have a brilliant idea to look less suspicious. I walk up to the water cooler near the hall and after I fill my bottle, I leave it there. This way, I can return for it. I saunter out from my room after a while with the pen in my satchel. This time, I feel less guilty. I walk into the meditation hall as if to fetch my bottle from the foyer and after quickly looking around to see if anyone is about, I replace the coveted pen on the clipboard. There is no pen on it and I feel remorseful, as if it was a precious, irreplaceable commodity.

I emerge from the hall, pretending to still be looking for my bottle. The whole charade is unnecessary and many weeks later, I shall find it comical, but in that setting and in that moment, it seems perfectly appropriate. I even enact an 'ah!' moment when I enter the recess and supposedly discover my missing bottle.

I walk back to the room, looking forward to sleeping after the sheer mental exhaustion of the act of returning the pen. It is as if I am unburdening by letting go one at a time; first, the focus on the book, then the notes and lastly, the pen. I collapse gratefully upon my bed on my back and cover my eyes with my arm to block out the light which filters in through the curtains.

N has gone away as if she never existed and I will never be able to ask her what plagued her, unless I manage to write my book and she traces me through it. I would have liked to help her; I know I could have. N is not the only one who has left, but I will discover this fact later.

In the afternoon session, we are told to continue concentrating on sensations on the philtrum. My mind drifts, but the thoughts are not about regret, pain, shame and sadness. I can even examine unbearable pain with an objective eye.

After an hour, the male teacher announces that we will now receive instructions for vipassanā. I am breathless with anticipation. The day did not seem to be going anywhere and suddenly, there is a prospect of a very big change. Although racked with pain, I am eager for the unravelling of the biggest secret; the fountainhead of strength. He tells us that we will not be allowed to change positions now and I become rigid with fear. Being ordered to not move is frightening. Guruji reiterates the same thing through the tape. I start palpating. I am already fighting waves of agony and it has barely been ten minutes since the start of the session.

Guruji's instructions are too swift for me. Suddenly that soft, unhurried voice is as if it is making up for lost time. I have a hard time comprehending what he is saying. He tells us to start observing sensations on the tops of our heads: the place where a baby's skull is the softest at birth and then to move down. I do not know which area at the top of the head he is talking about or how to start looking for sensations there. My mind goes back eleven years to when my son was born. I remember feeling a soft, vulnerable depression on his head, but my pain-racked body, the ordeal of the past four days and a complete alienation from the world outside has rendered me unable to pinpoint it.

Even as I am trying valiantly to home in to that spot, Guruji has moved on to instructions regarding the face, shoulders and arms. For three days, we have attuned ourselves to sensations only on the philtrum and suddenly we are required to feel every square inch of our bodies. Guruji has moved down further to the neck, chest, abdomen and the back. It seems like everything is happening in fast-forward mode. The sheer effort required to keep up with the instructions when I can feel nothing in any part of my body and the overwhelming physical agony of not being able to move has transported me into another world; a world which resembles hell.

I cannot hold out any longer and I open out my legs and tilt my body sideways. I feel broken, physically and emotionally. The agony does not abate. My whole being is still on fire, ready to explode. When it gets over and Guruji starts singing, I start to wonder if it is possible for anyone to go through this kind of torture in the quest for liberation. I am no longer indefatigable but a helpless, fragile being with an overwhelming urge to cry. I stand up on legs which do not feel like mine anymore. I need a place to vent the feelings of being in a hopeless struggle against sorrow. I do not know where to head; there is not enough time to go to the room before I dissolve into tears. I spot the pagoda and suddenly, uncaring of rules and regulations, I head down the shrub-lined path.

I walk fast now, fuelled by anger and frustration at having been unable to surmount the challenges which life has thrown before me. For some reason, a girl who is always dressed in a pair of flared pants also starts to walk down the path to the pagoda behind me. I do not expect that she will enter the pagoda. Opening the two sets of doors and heading quickly down the passage to the right, I open the door to one of the cells. Just then, I hear the main door of the pagoda being opened. I am stupefied at the thought of the girl having followed me inside but I am beyond caring. She will not be able to find me in this cell, one of countless others. The door is not locked but ajar and I hope she will be too unnerved by the sight of the dark passage and forbidding cells to want to try and explore or look for me. I sit down upon the cushion and closing my eyes, let the tears flow freely while a soft keening sound emanates from the depths of my being. I am letting out all the pain and strain of the past four days and of many wasted years before that.

I hear footsteps outside the cell and am amazed at the brazenness of the girl who has followed me right up to it. I feel a surge of anger but it is quickly replaced by mortification and a silent supplication that she will leave a helpless woman to her sorrow and go away. The footsteps walk away and die down. I have probably been heard and I feel ashamed at my display of weakness but I console myself in the hope that a fellow human being will understand an outburst of sorrow, for whatever reason it may have occurred.

The tears stop after a few minutes. I am ashamed to emerge from the pagoda with my teary face. I emerge out into the sunlight and look up at the bright skies to dry out my eyes and remove the pallor from my skin. I feel defeated, but I must go on. The ordeal is not yet over. In the dining hall, the searing pain of memories strikes me with full force to add to the self-pity and feeling of failure. The strength of the past three days seems like a chimera now dissipated by the harshness of reality.

There is a bulletin board outside the dining room. I am surprised I have not noticed it before today. The heading on a notice of the word ADHISHTAN has caught my attention. *Adhishtan* means determination and the notice says that since today we are going to receive the divine light of vipassanā, we must now determine to remain immobile for the duration of an hour each time, three times a day. This is the first time I realize that there are three adhishtan sittings in the day when it is imperative for us to be present in the hall. Seeing the diktat in writing makes me break out into a cold sweat.

I have no strength today to wash up and then head outside for the customary stroll before the evening session. I lie in the bed and let the waves of sorrow wash over me. I rise when the bell tolls. I do not know what is in store for us now, but I suspect we will undergo the same agony as in the last hour of meditation. To concentrate on sensations throughout the body is a new experience and to have to do that while battling untold pain is a mammoth task, beyond anything I have ever experienced.

Guruji commands us to perform the same Herculean feat of observing sensations on different parts of our body in the ordained order and to remain calm while doing so. This time, I am determined not to move, even if it kills me. I start from the portion of the head, which I think is the one we ought to start from and try to 'feel' it. Guruji is telling us not to linger on any body part for more than a couple of minutes and I have barely started at the top of my head when I realize I must move down. There are feeble sensations which I can now pick out; of cold, heat, pressure, numbness, tickling and pricking and even pain, though, surprisingly, as I move from one part of the body to another, the awareness of pain is the least prominent. This knowledge is surprising, as my body is awash with pain.

My back is breaking with the effort of holding it straight. My legs have already crossed the threshold of pain several times and I feel intense pain in my right knee. I do not remember ever enduring such extreme agony in silence; even though my children were born with the accompaniment of full-throated screams and cries. Still I sit motionless; determined to see this through as I know I cannot hope to reach salvation without following these demands of meditation. I have reached my left thigh in my exploration of sensation, after trying to explore my arms, neck, chest, abdomen and back; in that specific order. I have no idea whether we have to explore our nether regions as well, and I leave it out. My breasts go unexplored too; somehow, they do not fit into the equation at this stage.

Just as I am determinedly trying to 'feel' the top of my left thigh, I begin to lose hope and courage as the agony has now reached extreme proportions. I feel I am about to wilt and die. My mouth opens to let out a scream of anguish. It does not come, because a stupendous miracle happens instead. There is a huge lightning like jolt and a flash and crackle inside my body and all the pain disappears, leaving me completely limp. It is as if a spirit has been exorcised from my tortured physical form and the demons of suffering have been pulled out, twisted and contorted and screaming. A soft, calm voice speaks in the deafening silence and tells me nothing will ever harm me again.

A 'white light' has set me free. I cannot quite describe the experience of that sudden transformation from supreme and uncontrollable agony to a state of painlessness. For four days now, I have been enduring untold pain constantly. To be set free from it in this fashion is unfathomable and it renders my body as weak and pliable as that of a newborn child. I knew I could not hold on for even another second but divine powers intervened and made the pain disappear in a flash. The experience overwhelms me and I start sobbing uncontrollably, oblivious to my surroundings or the moment.

Blinded by tears, I reach into my sling bag for my handkerchief and sob into it with low, racking sobs. This is the moment I was waiting for; the moment when the demons would leave my soul. Guruji carries on with his instructions, but I do not pay attention, as I have already reached the higher realm. The secret has been revealed to me. Human suffering is temporary. When we can endure no more but still persevere, despite the certain futility of further endeavour, divine grace intervenes and years of needless suffering are taken away in an instant. I know my struggle and endeavour have been rewarded and there will be no more pain.

I lift up my face and look around me, expecting to see several others experiencing the same miracle. All I can see are contorted faces and closed eyes. No one is weeping and no one seems to have heard my sobs. I look at the teachers. Their eyes are closed, too and they seem oblivious to the miracle that has taken place with me. My eyes grow wide in amazement. I seem to be the only one to have undergone the divine experience. I feel a tremendous feeling of gratitude at having been the Chosen One. I have been supremely blessed, unlike any of the others and I know it is a result of my strife and the extremes of pain and sadness I have contained within for the past few years.

Maybe the enlightened teachers have noticed, but are not showing any sign of it. Maybe they are smiling within that one of their pupils has succeeded so beautifully and so soon. Still reeling from the intensity of what I have experienced, I know I cannot continue sitting in the hall and for the first time since the beginning of the course, I stand up on firm and strong legs and leave the hall.

I glance at the clock before leaving. There is hardly any time left for the discourse so I walk towards the mini hall. It is not every day that one experiences the benediction of God in the tremendous manner I have just experienced and the whole world seems wondrous. There is a peacock on the roof of the meditation hall and it looks like a sentinel: a silent spectator to all the wonders the meditators experience here. I feel kindly towards the peacocks now, that have been disturbing my meditation with their calls. The whole purpose of the meditation is to be able to concentrate even in the face of distractions. I really have lived a lifetime in the last four days. *This experience would make for such a wonderful passage in my book!*

I feel very alone at being unable to share the experience of the 'white light' with anyone. There is no use of such miracles without any witnesses or audience. I long to tell my soul sisters that I am gloriously free of pain; the state of painlessness probably being everyone's coveted goal as of the present moment. But I will necessarily be alone in my discovery of Divinity and God's grace.

I reach the mini hall and lean against the water cooler. The enormity of the experience brings tears to my eyes again. Once again, sobs emanate from the core of my ignorant being. I cannot understand why I had to suffer if God was eventually going to obliterate all pain. Maybe the suffering was required to mould me.

Unfortunately for me, the female teacher, who never comes to this side of the mini hall, appears in front of me. I am shocked and ashamed that she should see me crying; then I am relieved as if I expect her to come and enfold me in her ample bosom and praise my effort. I could do with some maternal comforting from a motherly figure such as my teacher. I bury my face in my handkerchief. She does not pause and appears not to have noticed me at all. I hear her enquiring something in the dining hall while a fresh cascade of tears roll down my face. She comes out after a few minutes and goes away, without even glancing in my direction. I dab my eyes. The other meditators will be here soon.

Since I have reached early, I occupy a place against the wall. There are only two cushions there and they are usually occupied quickly. I don't really need the backrest today as I have no pain, but these seats are coveted and I am still avaricious.

There is something different in the air here tonight; it is ponderous and heavy. I imagine everyone is thinking pretty much the same thing: how they will handle what is to come. If it has been so difficult for me, I imagine it has been no easier for anyone else.

The rains today have brought out insects and reptilian life by the hordes. There are numerous small frogs and countless beetles scurrying across the floor of the hall. There are many muted shrieks and jumps. There is a fat girl, who I shall refer to just as the 'Punjabi', who is more squeamish than the others. She jumps up in fright as a large frog hops behind her cushion and almost onto her back. I chase the frog out with a few waves of my handkerchief and calmly sit back on my cushion. The girl and I do not even exchange a glance.

The television set is switched on. I listen attentively today. I expect Guruji will ask today how many of us experienced the promised miracle and I feel a surge of pride. He starts without any preamble and tells us that the fourth day is very important (he does not pronounce the 'r' in important and the 'o' is also soft, so that it resembles the taboo word for men) because we have started the practise of vipassanā. He says that this is a very peculiar form of meditation. We generally view meditation as contemplation, reading of scriptures or concentrating the mind by verbalizing some name or word or visualizing some imaginary shape or form, but such meditation does reach the depths of the mind. Defilements are like large trees with deep roots, which remain even when the trunk is cut off. Today, he says, we have taken a dip in the Ganges of Dhamma. Throughout our lives, we have always given predominance to external objects without observing what is happening within; now, we would experience reality through *vedanā* or sensations.

Guruji discusses various questions relating to the technique of vipassanā. He explains why we need to move our attention from head to feet in a definite pattern and not randomly. It is because we need to keep our attention from getting diverted to those parts of our body which are experiencing the most intense sensations. This would cause the mind to remain 'gross', and we would not be able to reach a point where we would feel subtle sensations all over the body.

He says we might be exploring one part of the body and suddenly experience intense sensation on some other part. Should the mind be diverted to that part? The answer is no, because the purpose is to train the mind to observe subtler sensations. As to how long we should focus on a particular area to feel sensation, Guruji tells us that it should neither be too long nor so quick that one is through with the entire examination of the body in a second. There is laughter for the first time since the start of the discourse. Guruji smiles and says that one should take roughly ten minutes from head to feet during the examination, but taking a little longer is also fine. Also, the area to be examined at a time should be about two or three inches. I am glad Guruji is explaining the technique, for there has been a fair amount of confusion regarding it.

Guruji says we should work only with surface sensations for now. His usage of the word 'work' makes me think of blacksmiths with anvils, except here the blacksmith is the mind and the body is the anvil. Within ten days, he says, we might reach a stage where we will be able to penetrate inside our bodies. What he says sounds impossible.

Guruji tells us we will subconsciously be looking for something special in the way of sensation; something blissful or ecstatic. However, since we would keep experiencing intense pain, we would get disheartened. We would all be looking for 'something', without realizing that the 'something' already existed. We would also find 'blind spots', but this would only be because we were not yet advanced in the technique. If, however, we continued to focus with a balanced mind, the blind spots would go away.

He advises us how to pick up sensations. He says we could try to feel the touch of cloth or 'atmosphere'. At no time should we react, as the entire purpose of the technique is to change the habit pattern of the mind. He explains that the part of our mind which we consider 'unconscious' is not really so; it feels sensations throughout the day and keeps reacting. The one thing that becomes absolutely clear to a student of vipassanā is the reality of change. The fact that everything is a melting pot, that there is no substance anywhere, and that whatever happens is because of cause and effect.

Guruji now tells us a story. The direction and moral of his stories is usually apparent right in the beginning and this amuses me. The story is about a man whose father passes away. The distraught man begs the Buddha to ensure salvation for his father's soul. The Buddha tells the man to get two clay pots and fill one with stones and the other with ghee (clarified butter). The man eagerly obliges. The Buddha then tells him to immerse the two in a pond. Then he is told to break them open with a stick. Apparently, there is an Indian belief that when the skull of a dead man is broken open, his soul is set free and he can enter the gates of heaven. The man breaks the pots and the butter floats to the top, while the pebbles sink. The Buddha then says no rituals or beliefs can alter the course of things. As you sow, so shall you reap. Only an enlightened soul can be set free.

Guruji smiles and says with a little shake of his head that India is a land of great diversity. On the one hand, there are people like the Buddha, the one with supreme enlightenment and on the other hand there are people, like the ignorant man, who believe that one can bend the laws of nature through rituals, prayers and sacrifices. The only thing which yields fruit is our actions: physical, vocal and mental. Depending on invisible powers does nothing.

We also give more importance, Guruji says, to vocal and physical action without realizing that mental volition is very important. Everything originates in the mind. Vocal or physical actions are only yardsticks to measure the intensity of mental actions. The realization of an enlightened person is that the mind matters most. It precedes everything. We may use the same words to castigate a person we are angry with and for a loved one who has done something foolish, for example, a grandchild who has dirtied his clothes. The words and vocal action will be the same, but they will have different mental volitions. He further illustrates this with regard to physical actions. A murderer plunging his knife into his victim and a doctor plunging his knife into a patient's body will be similar physical actions, but one will be to kill and the other will be to heal. Nature takes mental volition into account, not the consequent physical action.

Guruji talks about the four parts of the mind: *viññāṇa* or consciousness, *saññā* or perception, *vedanā* or sensation, and *saṅkhāra* or reaction.

Viññāṇa, he explains, is the part of the mind which is responsible for cognizance. We have six senses, so there are six separate viññāas. Saññā is the part of the mind that recognizes the stimuli received by the senses and evaluates them based upon past memory. Vedanā is the sensation that is generated in the mind based upon the evaluation or saññā. If, for instance, one hears words of praise, there is an unconscious reaction of a pleasant sensation in the body.

Saṅkhāra is the only part of the mind which generates fruit, because it is the habit pattern of the unconscious mind, which results in a reaction of craving or aversion depending upon the kind of vedanā generated. The quality of saṅkhāras generated is very important and decide one's quality of life. There are three types of saṅkhāras. One is like a line drawn on water – there one instant and gone the other. The second is like a line drawn on sand – there in the morning and gone by evening. The third type is the most dangerous, it is like a line etched on a rock and it takes years to fade, if at all.

I love the analogy: lines which are drawn on sand and those which are etched on rock. In my life, I have drawn lines on rocks towards people who have instilled deep sorrow into my heart. I wonder if they will ever go; but the knowledge that our mind has the power to recognize and prevent those lines is there now. What I choose to do with that knowledge is up to me. How much easier life would be if all lines were drawn upon water.

Guruji says if we try and remember all those saṅkhāras we have generated during the course of the day, we will not be able to remember more than one or two. At the time of death, he says, there would be only one or two deep saṅkhāras which would come to the surface. Death is a morbid and incomprehensible subject for me and I feel uneasy when Guruji refers to it. I can think of only one saṅkhāra, which may come to mine at the time of death: regret. A lot of our life is about regret. What Guruji says next perplexes me. He says the state of the mind at the time of death is the state of the next mind which is born from it. Does this mean that vipassanā believes in the reincarnation of the soul? But Guruji is not talking about the soul; he is talking about the mind. It doesn't make sense.

I have never believed in the afterlife. In any case, I am here to better my current life. What happens after I am no more and who inherits my mind is irrelevant.

Guruji tells us that we must learn how to die. If all of us could live life with the constant acceptance and realization of death, the quality of our lives would be far better. Guruji is smiling serenely now. He says vipassanā meditators do not die unconscious. They do not die crying or fearful. He says they see death coming and say it is getting closer and closer and then announce that it has come! He spreads out his hands and brings them nearer and nearer to his body to illustrate this and smiles broadly when he says the words 'it has come'. There is loud laughter and even applause from the audience. Although Guruji's actions are funny, I do not feel like laughing.

In a softer, gentler voice, he says that the art of dying is perfected by the art of living and the art of living is what we are learning here. Immediately, I think of our spartan quarters, the frugal diet and the physical and mental hardship of meditation. Yes, we are learning the art of living here. He says we are here to change the habit patterns of our minds. There will be a constant lament against the immense pain and questioning of why we are here, but there will be a few brief moments when we will be able to bear the pain and fortify ourselves to not be averse to it. Those few moments will lengthen and become more frequent; and those moments will be wonderful.

Guruji tells us that the remaining six days are very valuable and we should make best use of the time. He sounds very sombre when he says we should endeavour to free ourselves of bondage and become liberated by not generating saṅkhāras. He chants 'bhavatu sabba mangalam' and the mandatory 'sadhu' is recited thrice in response by his television audience.

I head back to the meditation hall feeling more isolated than ever. I am alone in the conquest of the self and in being the recipient of a miracle. In the meditation hall, there is a slight tremor of rebellion when I assume the cross-legged position, but the fiery pain is missing. I can concentrate better on sensations on the surface of my skin now that I do not have to think about pain. But Murphy's Law dictates that a state of painlessness will be directly proportional to the shortest meditation period and soon the bell rings to announce the end of the day for us.

As I walk slowly towards the residential block, I look for aeroplanes in the sky. I spot one on the horizon. I do not stop to stare. It is like a precious memory in one's heart, like the face of a beloved, whose lines and contours have been imprinted forever in the mind. Maybe the universe is both ever-changing and constant; both finite and infinite. I am not wise enough to answer all the questions.

I see N's locked door and I cannot shake off the sadness when I think of her because she left the meditation course midway. She will also stay with me forever, as a memory or as an epitaph.

After entering my room I wash my face and change. I set up the mosquito net but then remember the wire netting on the back window. I have forgotten about the recess the window ledge may provide for skulking creatures. I look fearfully at it through the folds of the mosquito net, expecting to see a lizard hiding there. I cannot quite make out anything on the netting because of the light falling on to it from the room. I switch off the light and then peer again. The ambient light from outside falls eerily upon the netting but I can now see there are no creatures upon it.

I creep inside the mosquito net and wait for sleep, but the wonders of the day make me lie awake and ponder and marvel. Though my body is hurting once again, I expect it won't be long before I once again experience the 'white light', which will take away the pain. I feel very powerful. Slowly, my mind starts debating the existence of God, even though earlier in the day, I have been grateful to the Supreme power for the miracle today. I wonder if all those months and years spent in the pursuit of religion were worth it. If vipassanā is so powerful, why did I waste so much of my life on prayer? Suddenly, in the darkness of my room, I hear a voice saying, 'Who do you think sent you here?'

I am startled out of the cavalcade of thought. Was it really a voice I heard, or was it my imagination playing tricks? Is it God who has made it possible for me to find my strength by sending me here? How could I forget that we are given our trials and ordeals in order to be able to learn? Suddenly, the clash between faith and ego is gone. God gives us pain but then also helps us walk upon the path to succor. He is omnipotent. There is no need for me to give up my faith. The Almighty is still there, looking down upon me.

I fall asleep, satisfied that I am still a protégé of my God. Some time in the night, I find myself writhing in pain with a flash of light which courses like lightning through me. It is similar to the 'white light' except that it does not take the pain away but leaves me contorted and twisted for a few moments. I cry out silently, begging for deliverance. However, tiredness takes over once again and I fall asleep almost immediately after.

6

THE IRREPRESSIBLE LONGING

❧❦❧

Day Five

$\mathscr{I}$T IS RAINING. I DRAW ASIDE THE TINY LITTLE CURTAIN at the window facing the courtyard and see that it is nearly quarter past four. I am horrified and mortified that I should be so tardy. My first thought is of the sevika, who must be feeling triumphed if she saw my room in darkness at this hour. I hate to dress hurriedly and not be able to savour a few moments of daydreaming early in the morning. My body hurts. I remember the 'white light' last night. It has left me in as much agony as before. And I know only too well what hardship is in store. My stomach is empty and hurting from lack of food and since there was no fruit to take back at tea time, I do not have anything to assuage the hunger. I must ask for dinner from today.

A more morose figure could not have ventured forth from the block. It is dark and forbidding to walk even the short distance to the meditation hall. The path is wet, though not slippery.

As I sit down, I hunch with pain and the torment starts again. I have an overwhelming craving for tea. Maybe it is because the rain has made me cold. The thought occurs to me that I could bear the pain if I could only have some tea. I cannot concentrate on anything but the thought of drinking tea at breakfast and I can almost smell its aroma and taste its bitter sweetness. I open my eyes. There is a heavily overcast sky and it is still drizzling. I feel a bleak sense of foreboding.

When I step outside the dining hall, I look again at the bulletin board. In the notice about Adhishtan, it is written that we can choose a convenient and comfortable pose for the mandatory sitting of an hour. I am confused because I thought the cross-legged pose was obligatory. I am also relieved, though, that I can chose the most comfortable position in which to meditate.

The rain has stopped and a weak but glorious sun is making its appearance. I feel rejuvenated with the rays of the sun. As I bathe, I become aware of soft, soothing dohas being sung by Guruji in the distance. The sound is hauntingly beautiful.

In my room, I reach for the mosquito net. Suddenly, I am accosted by the vile and repulsive sight of a huge green grasshopper on the net. I recoil as if I have been shot. *Grasshoppers are not lizards, I cannot obviously sweep it away or frighten it into submission.* Trying to remove the netting will make it jump, probably in my direction. There is only one solution, I decide, almost weeping with the challenges thrown at me every day. I have to lift it and put it out. I pick up my handkerchief and slowly bring it over the grasshopper. I close it around the patterned yellow and green body. I then reach for the door and fling it out into the courtyard. The creature, unharmed, lands on the ground and no crow comes and takes it away. After a few seconds, it flies off. I am shaking. I feel alone and afraid, but also victorious. I am glad the creature was unharmed.

I generally use the remaining time to stroll outside but today I decide to stay and sweep my room. The dohas have just stopped playing in the distance. As I am sweeping, I spy the sevika in a room at the end of the courtyard. I did not know that she stays in the same block. She is getting dressed. I look away.

The path from the block to the triangular walkway seems shadier and hemmed in because a lot of vegetation has sprung up with the rain. Everything looks fresh and wet. I am filled with wonder and my senses thrill to the sight and smell of the world after the showers. There is a carpet of tiny blue flowers on the side of the path. They are absolutely beautiful and I smile to myself with happiness. The peacock feather is eluding me, but I have not given up the search.

Instead of perambulating just around the walkway as I usually do, I decide to go further down the path till the dining room. There is no one around. When I reach the teacher's quarters, which lie midway between the walkway and the dining room, I notice a woman coming up the path. She is about twenty steps away. At that very moment, I notice a monkey scampering at full speed towards the woman. It has its eyes on her and I wonder why, since she is not carrying any food. Time seems to stop for me. The woman might be attacked if I do not help. I am afraid but compelled to act. I raise my umbrella at the monkey when it is just a couple of steps away and shout loudly. The sudden action stops it in its tracks and it reacts with the instinct of a cornered animal. It bares its teeth menacingly at me and looks ready to pounce. I am petrified that I am the hapless victim now, instead of the woman, who is frozen in her spot. I do not move but instantly conjure up the image of Hanuman, the monkey god. I supplicate to Him to protect me. The monkey and I stare at each other in a silent duel. Suddenly, its stance wavers and averting its eyes, it turns around and scampers off. The woman who I have saved seems ignorant of my bravery and moves on dumbly. My holy book has come to my rescue once again, in a place where I have forsaken it.

Shaking with fright, I enter the meditation hall. Remembering the notice, I assume a comfortable frog like pose, with one leg half sticking out on the side. A lot of the bravado has faded in these five days. Guruji's dialogues in the audio tape have become increasingly repetitive as he tells us over and over again to explore the body from head to toe. The position I have assumed is no more comfortable than the cross-legged one after the first ten minutes. The painlessness of yesterday is long gone. My back is on fire because of the huge rope of pain on the right side; there is intense pain in my right knee and the smaller chord of pain in my forehead is throbbing madly.

Guruji has said that everything is impermanent. He repeats the word anicca during each sitting. I understand the concept of impermanence but cannot understand why I feel the same sensations in the same places all the time. There are parts of my body which I simply cannot feel. The upper part of the torso is a completely blind area and so is my nether region. My breasts still feel as if they are not a part of my body. Guruji has told us to feel the touch of cloth if we cannot find any other sensation, but it has not worked for me. The frog leg position is unbearable now and I shift back to sitting cross-legged. It eases my body only for a few seconds. My right knee feels as if is tearing from within. Thankfully, I hear the voice of the male teacher announcing group checking.

I ache to share the experience of the 'white light', but I know that it would be very vainglorious to do so. The female teacher smiles and asks whether we are having any difficulty with the technique. There is a collective plaintive murmur from all three meditators. Each has her own tale of hardship. After the teacher listens to all the complaints without doling out any words of encouragement, she turns to me and asks me how I am faring. I look her straight in the eye and look for an unspoken exchange about my experience yesterday. I do not find any. For want of anything else to say, I tell her it is excruciating to sit immobile. She replies that the very fact we are here on this journey at such a tender age is a feat in itself. I start to correct her notion about my age, but vanity causes me to graciously accept the comment.

I ask how we should sit during Adhishtan, unconvinced now that we can really sit whichever way we choose. She says we should aim to sit cross-legged for the stipulated one hour, but not suffer unduly. This doesn't really explain things, but I nod my head.

After group checking, the male teacher announces that the new students can go to the pagoda to meditate if they so desire. My heart lifts and my spirits soar. The moment I have awaited ever since the beginning of the course has come. I am filled with trepidation and excitement. It is forbidding inside the pagoda but I somehow know it is going to be a great step towards self-actualization.

Ten or fifteen of us start moving towards the pagoda. I am glad to see my name on the wall now. I have been assigned a cell not far from the one I entered yesterday. All of them look depressingly alike in the long, narrow and curving corridor. I enter my cell and close the latch. I am alone and isolated from the world, ready for answers.

The short break and the walk from the meditation hall to the pagoda have given my body a bit of respite, but the small cushion feels very hard and painful. The coolness of the morning has long gone. I feel the full force of the heat in the closed cell. Its only opening is the little circular window through which no draught or breeze comes in. I fight a feeling of nausea.

I am nervous about the fact that there is no clock here to tell me the time. But I know I will be able to hear the soft ringing of the bell inside the pagoda. I just have to close my eyes and sit out the hour. I close my eyes and try to concentrate, but I keep hearing footsteps in the corridor. There are coughs and even a few murmurs. Cell doors also open and close noisily. I am completely distracted and this unbalances my mind.

Willing myself to disassociate from the noises and the cloying, claustrophobic feeling, I start exploring my body. The only sensation I can feel, besides the omnipresent pain, is that of wetness from perspiration. I can feel little rivulets running down my back and settling in the folds of my stomach. The heat is unbearable. Impulsively, I raise my arms and take off my tee and bra. I also undo the hook of my pants. A stray zephyr touches my torso and tries to cool down my inflamed body. I feel like a pagan. It is mildly titillating to be sitting half naked for meditation. In spite of the heat and the pain, I almost giggle at the wantonness. *I am creating what could be a mini scandal in the ashram.*

Just then, I view an opening in the door of the cell; just below eye level. It has four narrow slats through which anyone can peek in. The thought is horrifying and I start to reach for my clothes, but I seriously doubt there are voyeurs afoot.

I start to meditate. I do not know how long I do so, but the stifling, cloying air of the cell, the rivulets of sweat and the intense pain make it impossible for me to continue. I am also very uneasy about the slats. I resignedly get up on unsteady and aching legs and I put on my bra and tee. Grabbing my satchel wearily, I open the latch and head out into the corridor.

My door makes a groaning sound as it is opened and my flip flops resonate softly as I walk down the length of the cloistered corridor. There are many pairs of footwear in the foyer, indicating that the meditators are still inside their cells.

The first touch of breeze on my face and body feels like manna from heaven. I head towards the meditation hall. I need to know how long I have spent in the cell. There are many meditators inside the hall, who have chosen not to go to the residential blocks or the pagoda. I hesitate entering because of the whiney door. However, the urge to know the time overcomes the hesitation. I open the door and tiptoe inside. Only the male teacher is present on the platform; he is talking almost inaudibly to a man who is not a student. He does not look at me. Everybody's face is a mask of serenity and pure concentration.

I glance quickly at the clock and I am horrified to see that it is only quarter to eleven. Fifteen minutes less than the stipulated time. I withdraw from the hall, feeling very small and incompetent.

I am not very hungry. The break between breakfast and lunch is a mere four hours, which is a lot less than the six hour break between lunch and the meager tea. I feel hungry only at night and in the morning. As I eat, I observe the others furtively. An old lady with a hunch and a bow-legged gait makes her way to a table with her meal tray which is heaped with food. Her sari is tied high above her ankles. I stare at her shriveled arms, sporting glass bangles. Is this the kind of person I wanted prosecuted for violating rules? I feel ashamed and I wonder what problems ail the poor old woman at home that she has sought succour in vipassanā. I muse whether the lure of free food makes many poor people come to the ashram.

I also observe the Punjabi. She has a self-satisfied look about her. Her brisk walk does not show any sign of weariness and she carries a big flask with her, which she fills with tea.

After lunch, I inform the sevika in a quivering whisper that I need dinner. My voice seems to have gone even deeper into my being. She asks me if I need it so I can take my medicines. Medicines are discouraged here, unless they are for chronic or serious ailments. I reply that I cannot concentrate on meditation because of hunger pangs. She says she will ask the authorities and tells me to meet her at tea time.

I am a bit wary and apprehensive when I emerge from the dining room. The episode with the monkey yesterday has left me unnerved. I look around fearfully as if expecting to see hordes of them coming charging towards me. I cross the teacher's quarters mid-way between the dining hall and the residential block and envy her little cottage and scraggly garden. I think I see her moving around inside and I turn my head away. It is very difficult to pay obeisance when one cannot speak or gesticulate.

As I walk towards the water cooler near the hall, the heat haze in the air, the butterflies fluttering about and peacocks foraging lazily in the distance lend the place an atmosphere of deep serenity and somnolence. I have a momentary feeling of complete well-being.

It is noon and I have an hour to go for meditation, but I cannot sleep. Guruji has warned that the sixth day will be very hard and I brace myself for the worst with dread in my heart. The room feels claustrophobic and hot. I decide to stroll on the walkway, where it is always cool under the shade of the trees on the island.

On the walkway, I see a mother and daughter duo walking briskly. I wonder whether filial ties would not interfere with the demands of meditation, which is supposed to be a lonely quest. They don't seem to be suffering from any physical or emotional hardship and seem to be enjoying the afternoon walk.

The umbrella and water bottle are tiring me out. I place them carefully on the parapet of the triangle and walk on slightly unencumbered. The search for a peacock feather is a constant obsession. I notice that the island with the trees has been swept clean of grass and undergrowth stacked now in neat little heaps on the side. No wonder I have not been able to find my talisman!

As I traverse the walkway, there is no thought of the world outside and no thoughts of hurt or regret. There is a new paradigm of self, and old associations and events seem to have little bearing on my present life. I wonder if this is going to change once I leave from here.

When the bell rings, I do not immediately head to the hall. There are four hours of meditation ahead and I am in no hurry. My right knee does not seem to know the concept of impermanence. It throbs with unchanging agonizing pain so that I have to change position within ten minutes of starting meditation. My pelvic joints are also bearing down with tremendous pressure. The examination of the body is an exceedingly painstaking and slow process. Imaginary fingers have to explore ceaselessly for the unknown.

Repressed thoughts manage to creep into my mind. I remember moments from childhood: moments of despair, moments of exhilaration. I remember people who have been dead in my memory for over twenty years. I remember struggles and fears – most of them baseless.

A break is announced. I open my eyes and turn around to see the time in the clock at the back of the hall. It is two. There are three more hours to go. I wander out on unsteady legs, wondering when the saga of unbearable pain will end. I walk towards the water cooler. There is a swarm of wasps around it. They have probably been drawn to the wetness. Some meditators hang around at a distance, unsure of what to do. I sense the collective fear. Circumstances here have made us into lambs, meek and accepting. Yet, thirst must be quenched. I walk almost through the swarm to the cooler. Wasps are not bees, I recall, they attack without provocation. However, I do manage to fill my bottle. Other mediators start approaching the cooler.

As I descend the steps to the toilet, I spot what I have been endlessly searching for: the coveted peacock feather! It is lying on a step, a bit worn and misshapen due to the rain, but a whole peacock feather, nonetheless. I bend down with my mouth open in delight and amazement and pick it up as if it were a letter from a beloved long gone away and hold it against my chest. Then, with a fear of embarrassment at the thought of being watched, I hurry down the steps.

I have found my talisman. Imaginary tears stream down my face. I cannot cry, but I feel like I did after the incident of the 'white light'. The feather has given me strength to carry on with what seems increasingly like a losing battle. It is my sign from God that He is there with me in my struggle.

So far, I have not really been aware of the passage of time during meditation. But now, the wall clock in the meditation hall becomes my lifeline. Time has taken on a new meaning with the pain increasing each day. I subconsciously start timing my head to toe explorations and the frequency of pose-changing. My ears now strain to hear the words 'Anicca, anicca', which signal the end of a sitting of Adhishtan.

The four hours of meditation in the afternoon session seem like an eternity now. Broken up into four sessions of one hour each, they are simply terrifying. In the morning hours, we can head to the room or the pagoda, but there is no such respite in the afternoon.

I change my pose only once during Adhishtan now, but it takes me all of my strength and courage. My mind is constantly on the clock, imagining its hands moving slowly. Each minute is long and ponderous and seems to have the potential to divulge great secrets if only I can grasp it. But I am not quite there yet. My goal is to sit without moving. I watch the American enviously, forgetting that everyone's experiences and thresholds are different. We live our lives according to others' comfort, strength and resilience levels and not our own; constantly comparing and belittling ourselves for not matching up.

Five o'clock. The four hours have taken a massive toll on me. Even getting up from my cushion is an ordeal. I sit in the dining hall, feeling utterly miserable about myself, the ashram and the course. I feel a loneliness I have not known for a very long time. Suddenly, I am scared of the remaining five days and wonder how I will last. I wonder if N didn't do the right thing by quitting when she did.

I remember I have to meet the sevika. I have taken a long time today over my meal because I have been mulling, slouched over my tray. She beckons me towards a room adjoining the dining hall; it is a kitchen with male cooks inside. I feel uncomfortable in the presence of the men, as if I have been in a harem for years. I keep behind the sevika. A man steps forward to speak with her. She turns to me and asks if I have any container for carrying dinner. I shake my head. She enquires if I want a proper meal and I tell her I am just looking for a little something to assuage the hunger pangs. At this, she explains something to the man and he goes off. We wait silently and he soon returns with a little tiffin. He hands it to the sevika who then hands it to me. I feel like a devadasi, one of those women consecrated to god. The solitary lifestyle and the absence of speech and interaction with the opposite gender for just five days have wrought this change in me.

Food will be some comfort tonight. Nights are getting increasingly lonelier and more frightening. I reach the room wearily and take out the peacock feather from my satchel. I gaze at it for a long time. It is not particularly beautiful, but it is my hope and succour. I place it upright in a corner of the window ledge that faces the courtyard, where I can look at it every time I glance out. A pleasing thought occurs to me: peacock feathers are supposed to ward off lizards. The utilitarian quality of my talisman pleases me.

I open the tiffin carrier. It contains only two rotis and a little vegetable. I place it on my jar of cotton pads. The bell soon rings and meditators pour out of their rooms. I am near the steps leading down to the toilets when the sevika startles me by hurrying up to me breathlessly and extending towards me a pillow I had asked for. I do not know what to do. My room seems like a mile away to walk and I cannot possibly take it into the hall. Sensing my predicament, she tells me to give her my room key so that she can leave the pillow there. I hesitate as if I have valuables strewn all over my room. Guruji has told us that our attachment to things is never-ending. Even my meager belongings are causing me to worry.

I also worry that the sevika will snoop and spot the stolen pen under the blanket. We are not supposed to have any writing instrument upon us. Still, not having much choice, I give the key to her. She returns quickly, proving my fears baseless. I blush inwardly with embarrassment.

During meditation, the huge knot of pain on the right side of my back feels like a gigantic cobra, with its hood spread out; my back its unfortunate lair. I have tears in my eyes. I whimper silently. I could bear the pain in my legs and right knee if only my back would ease up.

I need to speak to the teacher. I am becoming desperate and fearful. I would prefer to go to the male teacher but I feel I would be setting a wrong example. So I walk up to the female teacher in the break. I know my agitation and desperation is apparent. There are tears in my eyes which I quickly swallow. I inform her that I am in tremendous pain. She gently questions me how long I could sit without moving, five days ago. Reflecting back, I realize it used to barely be five minutes. She says I have made huge leaps forward and should not get discouraged. I wonder again if she knows and suddenly, I share with her the experience of the 'white light'. However, the inability to express myself well in Hindi makes the whole experience seem like nothing more than a sudden disappearance of pain. The teacher nods her head when I am finished and says only that my meditation is going fine.

Feeling empty and dissatisfied, I walk out of the hall. I am afraid I will not be able to carry on. And yet I cannot leave. I reach the mini hall and find myself in close proximity with the other female meditators, who are waiting there on the road outside. The door has not been opened. I sense the awkwardness amongst all of us. We do not know where to look so we can avoid looking at each other. The girl with the orange nail paint is standing with her back to us and looking across the boundary wall of the ashram. I follow her gaze.

Right there before my eyes, are the Aravalis; a long and unbroken ridge of low blue hills. I had hoped to see them from the ashram and they had been there in the distance all these days but I had not known. It is the most mystical and breathtaking sight I seem to have ever seen. I stand transfixed, lost in time, transported back to a world which I left behind a lifetime ago; a lifetime which has forever taken me away from the reality I knew for thirty-seven years. I could stand here and gaze at those blue hills till eternity, but I meekly follow the rest into the mini hall when the door opens.

Guruji looks around unhappily at the audience seated before him, moving his head from side to side. I wonder what we have done wrong. Perhaps he is unhappy at the high levels of despondency, which must surely prevail at this time. He closes his eyes. After a few seconds, he opens them and says sadly that five days of the course are over. The next five days are very valuable. He says the meditators remain in a state of confusion for the first few days. He pauses briefly and the audience starts to titter and then laugh. I am puzzled at the laughter. Guruji says that they start feeling more confident as the days go by, by listening to the discourses, questioning the teachers and through their own practice. This alarms me. It has happened the other way round with me. My understanding, stoicism and strength have waned in the last five days.

Guruji says there is no Buddha above the clouds with a ledger, keeping a track of how many head-to-toe 'rounds' we do every day. We have to open the 'kingdom of heaven' within. By this technique of meditation, the barrier between the surface level and the deeper layer of the mind is bridged and this barrier had begun to break in our minds as well. Anyone who observed misery as misery, without reacting to it, became a noble person. Guruji smiles broadly and says this is what we have been doing for the past five days: observing the misery of sitting for one hour at a time. There is loud laughter and I smile, too.

Guruji says a meditator came to him once and said, 'Goenkaji, the whole technique is so nice; I love it very much and your discourses are wonderful; just remove the one-hour mandatory sittings.' Still smiling, Guruji says he would love to be able to do that, but the technique would not work without it. He says he is aware that after about forty-five minutes of sitting, every subsequent minute seems like an hour and that when we hear the word anicca, it is like freedom from bondage. I shake my head in wonderment at his keen awareness of our frailty.

Guruji explains that we have experienced both the misery of bondage and the happiness of liberation in these five days, but the ultimate aim was to learn how to rid oneself of the bondage of misery forever. He says it is very easy to maintain equanimity when everything is pleasant. One can only experience the joy of liberation by not reacting in the face of pain. He says students sometimes tell him they have actually started enjoying their pain because they have stopped reacting to it. We multiply pain by adding the mental component of it to the physical component. This is the first noble truth. One must observe pain as pain and not identify oneself with it. One can learn to do this by trying to find out the centre of origin of the pain and its area of influence and observe other sensations present along it. In this way, one can reach a stage of awareness where, along with the pain, there is an undercurrent of vibration all throughout the body.

As we learn to observe misery objectively, Guruji says, we go deeper and deeper into the second noble truth i.e., unwanted happenings are not the real cause of suffering. One keeps trying to change the external causes of misery, without understanding that external causes are beyond our control. What is the guarantee that those causes will not recur: that unwanted happenings will not happen again? Misery is not outside; outside are only sensual objects. Knowledge of the real cause of misery is the second noble truth and when the real cause is eradicated, one experiences the third noble truth i.e., there is no more misery.

Guruji says suffering starts from the moment we are born and stays throughout our lives. But it does not end with the end of life. *'Marnan bhi dukkha,'* (death is also a great misery), Guruji says, with a gentle smile.

The Buddha, he tells us, discovered that misery is made up of five aggregates: one is the material aggregate of the physical form, which is made up of the subatomic particles called *kalapas*. And the others are mental aggregates: the cognizing, recognizing, feeling and the reacting parts of the mind. These five aggregates make up one's personality. *Upadan* is the attachment or clinging that results in these five aggregates. There are four basic attachments; one attachment is towards the imaginary 'I', which one cannot really define. Was it the mass of subatomic particles or was it the four mental aggregates? The recognizing and cognizing part of the mind recognizes and cognizes and then dies. Was this the 'I'? Or was it the feeling part of the mind, which was temporary? The reacting part of the mind also reacted and then fell still. What exactly was the 'I', which was so important to all of us?

These are words of great wisdom. I imagine most of us are here because of some violation, imaginary or otherwise, towards the 'I': the 'I', which means nothing in the expanse and infinity of the universe.

Explaining attachments further, Guruji says that the circle of 'I' expands to 'mine'. If one breaks an expensive wristwatch, there is a huge sense of loss and sorrow. The sorrow and sense of loss is not for the watch; it is for 'one's' watch. No one cries over the breaking of a watch; the same watch if belonging to a friend evokes sympathy at best. The worth of the 'mine' does not matter. The deeper the attachment; the deeper is the sense of misery. This is the 'law of nature'.

Guruji says there would be no more misery if 'I' and 'mine' were eternal, but they are not. The 'mine' passes as we watch helplessly, and if the 'mine' remains, the 'I' passes away. A separation is bound to happen. I feel a cool flow of succour inside me. We are all so temporary and so is our pain. We will all finally be lost to the sands of time.

There is also attachment, Guruji continues, towards one's ideas and beliefs. We do not see things the way they are, but as we see them. Our skewed perspectives also lead to misery.

Guruji explains how the flow of life happens: *Tañhā pachya upādāna*, which means desires turn into craving and clinging (*pachya* means to cause); *vedanā pachya tañhā* – sensations cause these cravings; *bhasa pachya vedana* – contact causes sensations; *saraytana pachya bhasa* – it is the six sense tools which cause contact; *nāma-rūpa pachya sarayatan* – it is the combination of the mental and physical structure which gives rise to the six sense organs as soon as the life flow starts; *viññāña pachya nāma-rūpa* – the flow of consciousness causes life; and *sañkhāra pachya viññāña* – all mental volitions are responsible for the consciousness of the next moment. Each time a sañkhāra is generated, he says, consciousness arises. At the time of death, he gravely informs us, a very deep sañkhāra arises on the surface and with a strong push goes on to arise somewhere else. Thus, the flow of consciousness continues. *Avijjā pachya sañkhāra* – sañkhāras occur because of ignorance; not intellectual ignorance but ignorance at the experiential level.

Each link of this chain became clear to the Buddha during his experiment with bodily sensations. Because of ignorance, one generates saṅkhāras. Because of saṅkhāras, there is consciousness. Because of consciousness, a new life starts in mind and matter. With this mind and matter, six sense doors arise. Because of the contact with the sense doors, sensation is produced. Because of sensations, cravings arise. These cravings turn into deep attachments. Because of the deep attachment to the cravings, the flow of life continues. I think of Kahlil Gibran's words; 'life's longing unto itself.'

Guruji says that the *bhava* saṅkhāra, the saṅkhāra generated at the time of death is responsible for a new life. I still cannot understand this. The thought of death and some residual mental matter going forward makes me nauseous. These concepts and the difficult Pali words used by Guruji have also taken a toll on my tired brain. But Guruji continues, saying *bhava pachya jati,* which means that after death a new life begins; and because of this, *jati pachya jara, dukkha, marna sambhavanti*, which means every life necessarily has to pass through miseries of disease, old age, decay, unwanted occurrences and death. All kinds of mental and physical suffering arise just because one has been born. This whole process became clear to the Buddha and could become clear to anyone who went deep enough.

Guruji asks how one may break this endless chain of events. Life starts with *nāma* and *rūpa*, mind and matter. One cannot avoid this unless one takes one's own life. Suicide is not a good option, he says, because the volition of the mind at the time of taking one's life would be full of despair and desperation. The 'last mind' of such a life would be full of agony and thus the next life would also be full of agony. Sullenly, I mull on the fact that we should be worrying only about our present lives. Guruji asks if mind and matter should not be destroyed, where could one snap the link? Could one destroy the six sense doors? That would be impossible. Similarly, to destroy all objects one came into contact with would be impossible. Contact would lead to vedanā or sensation, which one could not avoid.

The Buddha realized that one could cut the link at the point of sensations. Normally, *tanhā* or cravings arise due to sensations; now only wisdom would arise; the wisdom that sensations are not eternal. The Buddha observed sensations to see how long they would last and discovered that they all eventually die.

This knowledge makes me hopeful of speedy and certain delivery from pain, which is why I will spend the next three days in hopeless anticipation.

Simply observing sensations without reacting to them, Guruji says, would reverse the whole process of multiplication of misery and the process of liberation would start. From the starting point of sensations, there are two paths: the path of misery which keeps on multiplying, or the path of wisdom through experience of the knowledge of impermanence. Every sensation should turn into paññā *or vijjā*. Then, there would be no more *avijjā* or ignorance and the chain would finally be broken.

When the entire field of ignorance is eliminated, there are no more saṅkhāras. When there is no more mental volition or reaction, the flow of consciousness stops. This causes the cessation of the flow of mind and matter. The sense doors cease to exist if the entity comprising mind and matter ceases to exist. This would block any more contact. There would be no more sensations, and cravings would cease to exist in their absence. There would be no more clinging and the process of 'becoming' would cease. *Bhava nirodha, jati nirodho* – there would be no more birth and there would be an end to life and the suffering associated with it.

These are deep and disturbing concepts and I am not sure I want to accept them. Am I here to ensure I am not born again or am I here for betterment of my present life? *Nirvana* and *moksha* are all very well, but all I seek is resolution of this lifetime. As if reading my thoughts, Guruji says that it is perfectly acceptable for us to not believe in past or future life. It is more important to accept one's present life, wherein every moment one is generating misery for oneself.

Guruji's voice drops a little. It is as if raucous evening is giving way to somnolent night, which it actually is. It is like his work is done. He has shown us the light and it is for us to follow upon the path which has been illuminated. He tells us we may not know it, but we have already started rising out of our misery. As he says this, I bring forth my pain to feel its force; it certainly does seem feebler and somewhat irrelevant in the face of bigger and more profound things concerning the universe, cosmos, life and death, rebirth, infinity and impermanence.

Guruji says that the 'law of nature' is such that when one stops generating sankhāras, old and deep-rooted sankhāras start coming up to the surface in the form of other sensations. If one continues to maintain equanimity, they lose their strength and eventually die. Maybe the 'white light' was a deep-rooted sankhāra being eradicated. I shudder.

Guruji sings the words the Buddha spoke on achieving enlightenment on a full-moon night.

Aneka jāti samsāran sandha vissam anibhissam
Gahakaraka gavesanto dukkhajāti punappunam
Gahakaraka ditthosi puna geham nakahasi
Sabba te phasuka bagga gahakutam visamkhatam
Visamkhāragatam cittam tañhā: nam khayamajjhaga.

Translated in English, these words mean:

'*Through the round of many births I roamed*
without reward

> *without rest*
> *seeking the house-builder*
> *Painful is birth*
> *again and again*
> *House-builder, you're seen!*
> *You will not build a house again.*
> *All your rafters broken*
> *the ridge pole destroyed*
> *gone to the Unformed*
> *the mind has come to the end of craving.'*

I visualize a beautiful, resplendent night with a full moon and the Buddha emerging from the depths of his mind after a period of ten days. I wish I could do the same. I recognize these words from the dohas sung in the mornings and they sound as beautiful now.

As one goes deeper to purify the mind, Guruji says, certain faculties become sharper and one such faculty is the memory of the past. The Buddha saw many past lives as he went deeper and deeper within his self. He realized that he had achieved nothing in any of those births except the journey towards an inevitable end. In many lives, he searched for the Creator in order to understand why the body keeps getting destroyed and reborn. In search of the creator of the body, he kept taking rebirth but experienced misery each time. His words on that night of enlightenment were words of the ultimate wisdom that it is the saṅkhāras which are responsible for a new birth. When there is no trace of craving left, there are no new saṅkhāras and thus no more births.

The idea of wanting to permanently destroy the body which houses the soul is disturbing. The world still holds a lot of pleasures for me despite the pain and the sorrow. And what of God – the Creator that the Buddha talks about – the One who would want us to suffer numerous, pointless births and who we choose to defy through this technique?

Guruji says we have a long, arduous path ahead of us, but even a thousand mile long journey begins with the first step. He says that if we take out even one ton of load from the hundreds of tons that we carry, it is good enough. We can then go back home a little lighter. Laughter follows this remark; Guruji smiles. The camera pans out jerkily and Guruji lifts up his hand in benediction. I lip sync 'sadhu' with the others and then we are all left with the blank image of the television set. Guruji is gone and the loneliness of the night kicks in.

I am so weary in body and mind tonight that I can barely sit still for the roughly forty minutes left of the last meditation session of the day. Just before the commencement of the session, I see the American going up to the male teacher with some query and I am envious. There is so much I want to ask; only I do not know where to begin. I seem to have lost my courage. I cannot wait to get back to the room and lie down. My mind is a mess of thoughts of rebirth, 'white lights', my unwritten book and the confusing technique, which does not follow the laws of impermanence.

No ants or bugs have got to the tiffin. I open it and eat the rotis and the vegetable slowly. My curtain is drawn; I do not want to be watched. I usually open it after I put out my room light, so that I can look out onto the forlorn and bare courtyard. I sometimes feel like a character in a sad movie, where the protagonist has been left alone in solitary confinement.

My stomach is full and I look forward to drifting away to sleep, but it does not come. All the pain and weariness in the world is not enough to halt the cavalcade of thought. The talk of rebirth and how we pass on in the universe has made me afraid; as if I am responsible for a lot more than I came here to accomplish. I feel very alone and afraid.

I lie on my back, willing the pain in my back to go away. It does not. I start mulling at all that can be accomplished with one's body. As an experiment; because I do not seem to be close to falling off to sleep, I start meditating in bed. This is the first time I have done this. I am surprised at myself; after ten and a half hours of meditation today, it should be the last thing I would want to do.

I do not follow the pattern laid down by Guruji. I choose body parts at random; I focus on different parts at whim. Each part that I focus my attention on seems to get inflamed as if I have touched it with a lit wand. It is an amazing and wondrous exercise. I do not realize it that night, but not being under pressure to pick out sensations brings them to the fore more easily. I play with my mind and body; making my mind flit randomly like a butterfly to various body parts and making them come alive. For the first time, I also feel the tiny pulsation of life in the folds of skin in my nether region.

While I play with my body, I hope to fall asleep. But my body and mind are too alive with the throbbing of their life force. I stop meditating and try to let my mind wander. Unfortunately, it wanders to a place very unexpected and very painful.

I start thinking of my little daughter. I have gone five days without really thinking about her; knowing that she is home with her granny. But tonight, I think of her with pain and regret in my heart. It has been months since I enjoyed her company; I have been lost in my own private world of thoughts. She has been around without me focusing on the fact that she is an amazing and extraordinary child. But what pains me the most is the memory of her keening at the gate just before leaving. She is very attached to me in her own non-clingy way and I feel helpless at the thought that she must have gone away with fear and apprehension in her heart. I remember begging her here in my room to be quiet when she was trying to offer me her coveted biscuit because she thought I might go hungry. I have been there for my children a whole lot without actually being there in heart and soul. My regret, coupled with what happened here five days back, haunts me and assumes a magnitude of terror. I want to run to her.

I think of her round, cherubic face and her beautiful peaches and cream skin. I remember her long, thick and lustrous hair. God has certainly been kind to her in creating her physical form. She is also a delightful creature who always bounces back after a setback; be it an admonishment or a personal failure. She is almost never sad for any length of time. There has been too little appreciation for this side of her nature. It makes me hugely guilty. I long to be able to see her and hold her and appreciate her. My mind goes to her soft, round belly; a protruding paunch that is the butt of many jokes: for some inexplicable reason, I long to touch it and feel its softness. It is a mad craving.

I want to leave right now. I have had enough of meditation and miracles. I want to go home to my daughter. Nothing seems as important as holding her and stroking her skin. How have I not noticed my daughter before in the way I am doing now? Every little part of her body is so clear in my mind at this moment. Everything will be alright if I can just go home to her. Nothing else really seems to matter anymore.

I haven't seen my son for months. He is in boarding school and I visualize him tucked away in his isolation and not being able to express his loneliness and fears. How could I abandon my boy this way? What must he be thinking just now? Would he be asleep, or tossing in his bed, plagued with worrisome thoughts, much as I am? It has been a long time since I connected and bonded with him. However, the thought of my daughter hurts more. I think of the worn sandals on her feet as she stood at the gate of the ashram.

Children are putty in our hands; malleable to how we want to shape them. They become like our playthings. And so often, we do much wrong, with them accepting the destinies and personalities we carve out for them. God may have made an error in judgement by letting us be parents of the little creatures who depend on us.

I am racked with pain and almost nauseous with misery. Tomorrow is the sixth and hardest day and my spirit has slackened to an extent that I toy very seriously with the idea of leaving. Only the thought of mocking derision from people back home holds me back and the very faint, very feeble hope that succour, deliverance or liberation may be around the corner. The notes for my book are gone and I will never be able to remember enough to be able to write it, but the throbbing pain in my forehead is testimony to the fact that I have not yet let go of it in my mind. It has all worn me out to an extent that I just cannot seem to revive my flagging and flailing spirit. I start to cry. The hot tears roll out silently but do not take away the sorrow and the ache inside. They are copious and wet my pillow and when I turn to my side, I can feel the unpleasant dampness.

The sixth day will be the toughest and I just may be forced to leave here and never come back.

7

EXPECTING THE WORST

❧❦❧

Day Six

$\mathcal{I}$ WAKE UP ON TIME WITH THE SOUND OF THE BELL, BUT rouse myself with dread. The day, not yet awakened, seems dark and scary and bleak. It is raining once again. A forlorn, haunting and wet courtyard and a forlorn, lost room with a forlorn, lost soul inside. I dress slowly today, in no hurry to reach the dreaded meditation hall. I love the rain, but here it seems to add to the obstacles which already exist. I walk with my eyes fixed on the path, fearful once again of slimy, reptilian creatures.

In the meditation hall, I sit with my eyes open and with my legs out. The uplighters are on and the teachers are in their places. The male teacher is sifting through some papers and fumbling with the cassette player and the female teacher is just sitting and observing the throng. I notice that there are a lot of empty seats in the hall. Soon, the light from the uplighters is dimmed and we start to meditate in the darkness of our minds.

The knowledge has finally dawned on me that the morning session of two hours is not an adhishtan sitting and I do not try to remain unmoving. Still, each minute ticks sixty seconds away slowly. When I hear the curtains being pulled open, I wonder if it is daylight already, but unlike yesterday, I do not open my eyes.

My legs are slightly wet due to the rain. There is an ache, because of the fan, which seems to penetrate right into my bones. I cannot even cover my legs with my immobile hands, folded in my lap. After a while the hand bell starts ringing. I unfold my legs and try to get some warmth into my legs with my hands. The ache refuses to go. The skies are still overcast and there is no sun to soothe them.

I sit in the dining hall with the cooler on at full blast as usual. I am not very hungry. My appetite has reduced because of the lack of exercise. I remember the tiffin and berate myself for not having brought it to the dining hall. I will have to return it at lunch.

I wash out my utensils and walk out. The dohas are playing, but the sound is not loud enough to jar. I feel like a permanent resident of the ashram. A part of me actually wants to stay here forever, even though the ache for my daughter has come back in full force. I find myself increasingly thinking about what she must be doing and whether she is missing me. I am tempted to go to the office and beg to call home just once to be able to get news of her and maybe talk to her, but I know that would be a gross violation of the rules. We never value people till they are gone and then we spend lifetimes aching over the loss, steeped in regret. This is true for lovers, for parents, for progeny.

I decide to wash some clothes today. It will be a break from my monotonous routine. As I wash them, I spy a few brown tick-like insects in one corner of the bathroom and am filled with revulsion. They look like ticks and I wonder if the red bumps on my body are there because of these bugs that probably make their way into my bed at night. I bathe hurriedly. When I wash out the floor with water thrown from the bucket, I try not to look at the ticks and pretend I do not know whether they have been washed away into the drain. Surely, one cannot be blamed for what one does not know and some things just cannot be avoided, like the lizard that was taken away by the crow.

The sixth day seems it is going to be as Guruji predicted. I wonder if the pain will be magnified to an unbearable crescendo. The overcast skies add to the worry and pessimism, and the feeling of dread and gloom.

I look across the courtyard at the clock and the women walking in after breakfast, while I comb my hair. They are seemingly oblivious to pain and sorrow and the demands of the course. I hear some of them talking and it disturbs me that rules should be blatantly flouted. I hang the washed clothes on the line. There is no sun yet. Fearing my legs will once again be cold under the breeze of the fan in the meditation hall, I look for something to cover them. All I have are some T-shirts and it would seem rather funny to carry one to the hall. Then I have a brainwave. I take off the newly washed pillowcase on my pillow and carry it with me to use like a coverlet.

I head out onto the walkway; the place of my great muse. Suddenly, a horde of monkeys come racing along from the side of the dining hall towards the residential blocks. I am directly in their path. Terror stricken, but also fortified with the knowledge that I have faced this threat before, I continue walking, tapping my umbrella hard on the ground. I display a confidence I do not feel. Fortunately, the monkeys seem either disinterested or wary and scamper past without incident. The mother daughter duo is out exercising and stand rooted with fear while the monkeys run past. I am breathless with fear but also proud that I have held my ground once again.

The vegetation is spilling over in its abundance and little wild flowers are everywhere in the undergrowth. The rain and the dampness under the still overcast sky have brought about several kinds of insects out onto the path. The most repulsive, but also the most fascinating, are big clusters of tiny red worms, sliding over each other constantly. I often stop to stare, in spite of myself. So do a lot of others. Maybe we just do not have enough time, inclination or opportunity to admire flora and fauna so closely in our dreary worlds outside.

I am dreading the next three hours of meditation. The knee and back pain lie coiled, waiting to spring up and unleash their power. I place the pillowcase on my calves. It is a relief to not feel the unrelenting breeze of the fan. Mechanically, I fold my right leg under my body when the pain gets unbearable, then I switch back to sitting cross-legged. The tendons and ligaments in my knee feel as if they are all worn away. My back is hunched with pain and I slouch, because holding my body erect is almost impossible now.

There is group checking in the next session. The others have their usual questions and grievances. The teacher just says to be patient and resilient. She always speaks in chaste Hindi and I am fascinated by some of the words. I resolve that I will study my native tongue once I leave the ashram.

When we are given the option to meditate in the pagoda or our rooms, I do not hesitate. I tell myself I will not succumb today to pain or fear.

I realize today that the door of the cell does not lock. The groove in the wall is too shallow to hold the latch. The knowledge shocks me. Just yesterday, I have sat here unclothed, thinking the door was securely locked.

We are required to explore our bodies in both directions now, top to down and vice versa. I have started completing one round in about fifteen minutes and change position in about thirty. Today, I want to cross that threshold. I am in the same agony that I was two days ago, when the 'white light' rescued me. Perspiring with the pain and the effort,

I carry on meditating nevertheless. Guruji is right when he says that continued observation makes one aware of sensations beneath the pain. When I examine the parts of my body minutely, I feel something else beneath the pain. This does not happen in my back, where the huge twisted rope of fire is too much of a distraction for me to examine it minutely.

In the fourth round of observation, I slump over. I have crossed my threshold; a tremendous feat to have accomplished and tears spill over from my eyes. A voice, very similar to the one which I heard when I experienced the 'white light', tells me to let go of guilt.

I have sat immobile for forty-five minutes. The pain does not recede after I change my pose, but the weeping has taken away some of the strain that has been there in my mind. If the sixth day is supposed to be the worst, I am not doing too badly. Threshold having been accomplished, I rise and head out of the pagoda.

I view the several pairs of footwear in the foyer of the pagoda sanguinely. A weak sun is out and as I walk through the patches of sunlight, warmth penetrates into my skin. Walking about assuages the pain a bit but my body still feels as if it has been through a mangle. My gait is even slower; I seem to crawl down the path to the rooms. I think about the voice in the pagoda. How many times has each one of us heard voices which have saved our souls by giving us hope, peace or succour?

I shift my washing further out on the washing line to catch the sunlight and then head towards the dining hall. I am late today. I hand the tiffin to the sevika, who asks me if I want dinner today as well and I reply that I do. I hurry with lunch because I need to wash my hair and then maybe get a little sleep.

After washing my hair, I start calculating the days left to go home. Today is the sixth day; I came here on the seventeenth of the month. This is a ten-day course. I am due to leave on the twenty-ninth, according to the schedule given prior to the course. It does not add up. Panic floods my being: N was right when she said she was afraid she might lose track of the days. I have no calendar and no dates are put up on the notices outside the dining hall. If today is the sixth day and we leave on the tenth, or rather, the eleventh day, it still adds up to only twenty-eight. I start palpitating in the cloying space of my little room. I feel like a prisoner who does not know when she will get her pardon.

I cannot ask anyone. What should I do? Suddenly, I remember the newspaper lying in my room. It is probably very old, but I can calculate months ahead if I have to. It is my only hope. When I pick it up, I am stunned to see that it is recent. The date on it is the fifteenth. I look at the day and calculate ahead to check what day I will be leaving from here. It is supposed to be a Sunday. But it still does not add up. I have to fight to keep my breathing normal and quell the surging panic. How has it gotten so mixed up? Why did I not just draw simple strokes on the wall of my room?

The confusion over the dates has amplified the stress I feel over my book. The recounting has not stopped. I step out into the courtyard very dejected and despondent. The pigeon atop the heater shifts and eyes me quizzically.

The sun is partly covered by clouds. The mother daughter duo is not about and I am glad I do not have to avert my eyes. There is a peacock in the undergrowth just a few feet away from where I am walking and I stop to admire it. But when I stand still, it senses danger and hops further away. I move on.

I have a new threshold now. Forty minutes of stillness. I have done it in the pagoda and now have to maintain that standard. My ultimate goal, though, is one full hour of adhishtan. My legs now feel disjoint from my body and I feel while sitting that I will never be able to walk again.

I remember being constantly scared that the immobility and numbness may cause some permanent damage to my limbs.

Loud sighs emanate from the meditators. Along with the sighs are coughs and sneezes. One male meditator has a terrible hacking cough and I wonder how anyone can meditate in that state. It is disturbing and I keep waiting for the teachers to send the meditator out, but it does not happen. The hacking sounds, the sighs and the loud and jarring calls from the peacocks perched atop the roof of the hall cause me great distress when I am trying so hard to ignore the pain and concentrate.

I manage to hold position for about thirty-five minutes, after which I shift unhurriedly, as if I am master of my destiny and my fate. My numbed legs take time to move and there is terrible pain when I do.

After two or three sessions of meditation, when I shift my legs, there is a faint and almost pleasant popping sensation and they relax briefly. I start looking forward to those seconds of relaxation. I also seem to be playing a game of snakes and ladders with my body. As I move my attention downwards, it 'slides' down the thick ropes of pain in my back and forehead.

I no longer bother to suck in my abdominal fat while I sit and meditate. Vanity has completely disappeared due to the demands of meditation. Also, most meditators here are very simple in dress and appearance; though I find many attractive. The old lady with the gold nose studs has beautiful features even though they would go unnoticed on a normal day. The American is not beautiful in the conventional sense, but she has grit and love and goodness on her face. I often observe the olive-coloured skin of the Italian – her plump and taut face is pleasing. The silver earrings, of course, steal the show. Even the girl in flared pants is pleasant. The happiness never seems to fade from her face. The girl with the orange nail paint is tall and lean and could make a good model, with her darkish skin tone and frizzy hair.

I muse that I might be a pleasing sight. I blush inwardly at the thought that my thick auburn hair might be a distraction. Stray wisps brush against my face. They tickle my skin but at this stage, external stimuli have become unnecessary to feel sensations. There are now vibrations below the skin, which flow to and fro on their own, often in continuous fluid movements. Guruji tells us that we should now try and feel body parts together. This, I realize, is happening on its own, especially in the legs. I no longer have to pause to examine them; there is an automatic energy flow right through the awful numbness and pain. How this energy can be present alongside the pain and pass through my numb legs is something I cannot understand.

There are other areas where I still have to struggle to pick up sensations. Each hour of meditation, I make the same round from head to toe and back, feeling the same pricking, heat, cold, tickling, itchiness, throbbing or pure energy flow running like a current down my body. All the while, the agonizing pain dominates.

It is with great tiredness that I finally rise from my cushion and make my way outdoors. It is sweltering. I unclasp the clutch from the strap of my satchel and comb out my hair with it. I like the feel of the slight breeze through my open hair. I am despondent, but the urge to quit is not overriding today. I expected the worst from the sixth day but the worst has not yet come. I make my way to the dining hall for tea.

I often long for pen and paper, but I know even if I was writing, I would still be memorizing each experience. Maybe the craving to remember would have been even greater. I might have been half way through my book by now, completely ignoring the demands of meditation. I have traded my book for my peace and liberation from struggle and pain.

I think about N today. I wonder where she is. Does she regret having left? In the face of the hardships and ordeals we are undergoing and the prospect of further mental and physical struggle, I wonder if she did not do the right thing. Each day here is equal to a lifetime.

A peacock flies up to a tree near the female teacher's residence when I make my way to the dining hall. I realize it is about to retire for the day. It settles on a branch which is probably its night perch and soon only a bit of its tail is visible. I smile at how well it is suddenly camouflaged. I would love to explore around more, but obviously I cannot venture into the grassy openness beyond the path. It might result in some serious castigation.

I ask for dinner again at tea time and walk back to my room with the tiffin tucked securely within the crook of my arm. Forlorn calls from peacocks make me sad and nostalgic, but it is a good sadness. I have almost made it through the most difficult day.

I glance at the notices outside the dining hall. One of them reads that the students can question the assistant teachers in the hall at noon every day. I register and store this piece of information in my mind for future use.

Once in the room, I draw the curtain on the window overlooking the courtyard and open the one on the window at the back. I look out at nothing in particular. I wish I had a more beautiful view at the back. Just then, a peacock calls out loudly. After some peering, I spy it in a big, sturdy tree just beyond the boundary wall of the ashram. Answering calls emanate from all directions. Maybe the tree is this peacock's home for the night. Are the calls the creatures' way of saying farewell to each other for the day?

The evening meditation before the discourse is always one of revelation and progress. Today, I try and look for undercurrents beneath the pain. The pain makes me almost delirious and I wish another 'white light' would deliver me from the agony. If only my legs would ease up, or my back. I could bear the pain in one. Two is impossible. I am not even considering the lesser pain in my knee and my forehead. Barely thirty minutes pass before I need to move. But I know now that the agony will abate only briefly before it once again consumes me. Nothing will help, unless I stop meditating. This knowledge fixes my body in its place like a stone statue.

The pain ebbs away slowly from my left leg. The numbness and pain are gone. The feeling is spectacular.

Just to have one limb free of pain makes a world of a difference and I can hold on for another five minutes or so before I unfold my right leg. I was right though; the pain ebbs only for a minute and then comes back. I have crossed another threshold and been rewarded with the knowledge that resilience leads to miracles.

Unfortunately, this is not the lesson we are here to learn through vipassanā.

The momentary relief and the sudden fluidity of movement in my left leg have given me much hope and succour. When the audio tape comes on, I slump in gratitude. When Guruji chants 'bhavatu sabba mangalam', instead of lip syncing the word 'sadhu' as I usually do, I say it out aloud.

The Aravalis are cobalt blue today. When will I leave this place? I have no idea and the knowledge fills me with helplessness and dread. I look at the low boundary wall and have a momentary fantastical vision of escape. This is actually quite funny, because if I wish to leave, all I have to do is continue walking down the path. It is only a few steps to the gate and to freedom.

We enter the mini hall and take our seats. I have placed a cushion against the back wall. I cannot sit without a backrest anymore for the discourse. There are a lot of little creatures scurrying around on the floor of the hall today; little beetles, little frogs and little bugs. The other women are terribly shifty and squeamish; I observe the insects and frogs dispassionately. When a creature gets close enough to amble up my foot or leg, I set it on a different course with a little flick of my finger.

The audio-visual comes to life. A message on the screen reads 'Day Six of the vipassanā course'. I feel bile rising up my throat because I do not know how many days are left to go. Guruji says he is glad this day is over. He smiles faintly. Surprisingly, there are titters from the audience. One of the biggest reasons for wanting to leave on the sixth day, Guruji says, is that the discourse on the fifth day is full of talk of misery. He is not joking, I think to myself. Consequently, he says, one feels pessimistic. However, the path would be pessimistic if it only talked about misery; on the contrary, it gave one a way out of misery.

He tells a story about a woman who sends her son out to buy a bottle of oil. On the way home, the boy trips and drops the bottle of oil. Half the oil spills. The boy comes back crying with the half empty bottle of oil. Here, Guruji interjects, 'A story is a story, so the mother sends out another son to fetch another bottle of oil.' There is another round of titters from the audience on screen and smiles from all of us watching. This son also falls down and drops the bottle. Again, half the oil spills out. The second son is an optimist. He tells his mother that he dropped the bottle, but managed to save half the oil. Continuing with another 'A story is a story, the mother sends out a third son to fetch the oil,' he says that the third son also spills half the oil, but, being a vipassanā meditator, he is both an optimist and a realist. He tells his mother he is left with only half the oil, but by evening, he will earn money and replace the lost oil. The story reminds me of the phrase 'glass half empty and glass half full'. It is not enough to simply accept loss; one can do something about healing or repairing it. I am full of admiration for the vipassanā boy and wonder how I can repair my own life.

Dhamma, Guruji explains, is not merely optimism. It is also realism and 'workism'. There is no trace of pessimism in Dhamma. Suffering is a part of life and one has to accept it. One has to work towards how to fill the half empty bottle. Guruji says we have started realizing the truth about suffering through observation of sensations. It is an observation of living truth. Craving for outside objects, we forget that craving makes us lose the balance of our minds. We also do not realize that we have become addicts to craving.

He gives the example of a man who has a one-bedroom cottage. He craves for a bigger house, so he buys a three-bedroom house. Then, he wants to furnish it with all kinds of gadgets and conveniences. The whole house, Guruji says, becomes so full of things that there is no space left to breathe. The audience laughs. Of course, all of us are only too familiar with the bane of our existence: our wants. Guruji continues that the man now craves a good car. He buys a Toyota, but then wants a BMW and then a Mercedes. Guruji calls the BMW a 'BWM' and I smile. Guruji says that even that is not enough for the man. He wants a Rolls Royce. When he has a Rolls Royce, he wants a fleet of them. After that, it is a helicopter and then a private jet and finally even a spacecraft is not enough to satiate his craving. I am reminded of the opulent and extremely extravagant lifestyles of the super rich. I have often mulled over how much is enough. Fortunately, I am not acquisitive by nature.

Guruji laughs and says that for a person like this man, the sky becomes the limit and even the sky does not remain the limit. This is in reference to the spaceship and I smile again. Desires become an endless bucket which cannot be filled. Craving is no longer for material things, but for the purpose of satisfying the addiction to craving. For people addicted to alcohol or drugs, it is not the substance, but the addiction to the sensations produced by them that cause the addiction. This was the Buddha's discovery: that one becomes addicted to sensations. Addiction of alcohol or drugs is nothing compared to the addiction to cravings or aversions.

I prefer today's discourse to yesterday's discourse filled with technical jargon; even though the vision of Buddha on the moonlit night and his enlightenment was hugely poignant. That vision will always connect me to unknown and unseen past lives and endless future ones. I will always be a mote in that infinity; unless, of course, I too am able to destroy the materials that have built the house: my body.

Guruji says we crave particular sensations and thus generate impurities in our minds. The process is repeated endlessly. It becomes the habit pattern of the mind and the way to break this vicious cycle is to observe: simply become a silent witness to whatever is happening without reacting to it – like a person on the bank of a river watching the flow of water. The entire physical structure and the entire mental structure and the combination between the two become clear as one observes dispassionately. It also becomes clearer how the two influence each other and how the mind originates because of matter and vice versa. Listening to all this excites me. It opens up the possibility of some amazing biochemical changes in my body which will alter my mind, or perhaps the mind will be a part of those changes. I eagerly await them.

Guruji says the physical structure and the universe are made up of the four basic elements of air, water, fire and earth and that all sensations are manifestations of these four elements. A feeling of heaviness or lightness in the body is a characteristic of the earth element. The entire field of movement within the body is a characteristic of the air element. The sensation of temperature is an expression of the fire element. The water element is characterized by a feeling of cohesiveness or binding. All sensations are these four elements manifesting themselves.

Like a scientist, a good vipassanā meditator explores the truth of sensations and the nature of kalapas or subatomic particles within the body and how the mind gets influenced by them. There are four factors that determine the kind of kalapas that will be generated: two are mental and two are material. The first physical or material factor is the food one consumes. For instance, one will feel heaviness or burning inside the body if one consumes hot or spicy food. The second is the input of the atmosphere around. Saṅkhāras constitute the mental inputs: saṅkhāras, which are generated in the present moment, and old saṅkhāras. The kalapas generated at the physical level because of anger will have a predominance of the fire element. A saṅkhāra of fear will have an element of air in the form of a reaction such as trembling. When no new saṅkhāras are generated, old ones start coming up to the surface and are eradicated.

Nīvaraṇas, Guruji says, are curtains that block the reality within. There are five big enemies or obstacles to meditation. One, of course, is craving. Guruji smiles and says we are not supposed to communicate with others during the course, but we just cannot resist observing and even asking others how they are progressing. On hearing that a meditator has been experiencing tingling vibrations throughout the body, we would be debilitated by craving. I sit up a little straighter. I have already experienced tingling vibrations in my body.

Guruji says if one keeps running after what is not there and saying, 'I want *nibbana*, I want nibbana' (nibbana being the state of 'unbinding' of the mind from mental effluents and the cycle of rebirths), one would not get anywhere and would, in fact, be running in a direction opposite to the desired one. Guruji says nibbana is a stage free from craving, but we crave for it. I am fascinated by the concept of nibbana. I will learn that it denotes cooling, peace and stillness. It is the final passing away of the *arahant*, one who is not destined for future births.

Guruji says we are not supposed to open our eyes during adhishtan, which he pronounces as adhitthana; but we cannot resist after about thirty or forty minutes and open our eyes to see how others are faring. There is loud, embarrassed laughter. Guruji smiles knowingly. He says we notice everyone sitting erect like Buddhas with eyes closed and wonder why we cannot do the same. We also wonder why our teacher says 'anicca, anicca' (everything is impermanent); when the pain is permanent. Once again, there are hoots of laughter, which slowly fade to titters while Guruji continues smiling. My smile becomes a broad, sheepish grin.

Guruji tells us another nīvaraña is drowsiness. The way to counteract this, he says, is to stand up, walk about or even go out of the meditation hall if the session does not demand adhitthana. This is news to me and I feel a faint twinge of irritation that we are not told this in the beginning. Another enemy of meditation, Guruji says, is doubt. Doubt about the technique and doubt about the Guru, who does not resemble the typical Guru with matted hair, shaven head and a necklace of rosaries and who generally 'does not look like a freak'. He says we might exclaim, 'He looks too straight!' and there are peals of laughter. Guruji is referring to himself. Certainly, Guruji confounded my expectations of a Guru. Not in his appearance, but definitely in his manner. I expected a Guru to be staid and serious and to only sermonize. This Guru tells stories which would enthrall little children and is full of self-effacing humour. This is a Guru who was not born to religion or spirituality. He is an erstwhile industrialist, who gave up wealth and ambition to propagate the teachings of the Buddha.

Guruji is still smiling broadly, enjoying the effect his words are having on the audience. He continues that we might think that this teacher seems to have no supernatural powers and wonder why his assistant teachers in the meditation hall keep asking the students how their meditation is going when they should automatically know everything.

The third nīvaraña, Guruji says, is doubt about one's own capability. Smiling, he mimics a meditator who says, 'This scene is not for me; I better run away.' The audience loves the histrionics and I smile, too. I will not be running away, even though I miss my daughter very much and my efforts seem to be fruitless.

Moving away from the discussion about nīvarañas, Guruji tells a story about a woman called Kissagautami who had a son after many years of being childless. Unfortunately, the child passes away at an early age and Kissagautami becomes nearly insane with grief. She refuses to give up the body of her child for burial. Well wishers finally send her to the Buddha. The Buddha knows that sermonizing to a woman so distraught with grief would be of no use. He tells her he will help her and orders her to go and get a few sesame seeds. The woman thinks this is going to bring back her son and agrees hopefully. The Buddha tells her the seeds have to be from a house in which no-one had died. Kissagautami goes from one house to the other but cannot find a single house in which no family member has passed away. Slowly, realization sinks in that loss is part of everyone's life. In the evening, she returns to the Buddha, ready to listen to his teachings. She spends the rest of her life helping others in distress.

Guruji recounts another story about a woman called Patacara who lost all her loved ones and became insane with grief. She roamed naked on the streets of a town called Savathi, unaware and uncaring of her shame. Maybe because of her past good *pāramīs* or spiritual qualities, she came into contact with the Buddha, who clothed her and taught her Dhamma. The Buddha did not give her back her loved ones; even if he could have, it would have been temporary, because life is transient. This truism hits me all of a sudden. Why do we develop attachments and cling to things when nothing lasts? Guruji says we live our lives with a great sense of loss. If we collected all the bones of those who had gone away from us in our present and past lives, it would make a huge mountain. Similarly, if all the tears of present and past lives were collected, they would make an ocean. Enough of suffering, Guruji says.

Guruji has yet another story. They are a refreshing change from all the profundity and morbidity of yesterday. Guruji says there was a very rich man who used to give a lot of *dana* or alms to make himself illustrious. In fact, the sobriquet given to him was Anathapindika, which meant giver of alms. However, it dawned on him one day that his wealth was only because of past karmas and thus should be used for the good of others: but it was no use clothing a person; once the clothes got worn out, the person would be naked again; it was no use feeding a person, the next day the person would be hungry again; alms alone would not alleviate misery – the dana of Dhamma was the greatest dana. He started looking for a place to construct an ashram in Savathi. There was no land available in the crowded city. He then came upon a lush garden, but it belonged to a prince who refused to part with it. Anathapindika offered to give any price that the prince quoted. Upon hearing this, the prince agreed to sell his land for enough gold sovereigns to cover every bit of his land. Anathapindika gave the prince his wish. The astonished prince asked Anathapindika if he was mad. Anathapindika replied that if all his wealth were to benefit even person, it would be worthwhile.

The ashram was set up and accommodated ten thousand people. One day, Anathapindika lost all his wealth and became a pauper. Whereas previously he used to take food and offerings to the ashram, now he had nothing to give.

But then he realized material offerings were not necessary. There was a fertile patch in his backyard, where many exotic trees and plants grew. Anathapindika took some of the rich soil to the ashram and grew a tree there, hoping it would provide shade to meditators for generations.

Guruji says mental volition should be good, whether it is with a million rupees or with a handful of soil.

It is a beautiful story and very inspiring. One can do wonders with almost nothing; even with the shreds of a soul torn into pieces.

I walk back from the mini hall in the dark because the lamps on the path are unlit for some reason. It has been drizzling and the path is wet. There are soggy leaves on the ground. I wait dejectedly for the discourse to finish. I need to talk to the teacher again. My forehead hurts all the time and I am worried that this might be related to my great and unfulfilled desire of a book.

I eye the numerous grasshoppers outside the meditation hall warily. I don't have the resilience to brave them tonight. The seven soul sisters stand a little apart from each other like strangers in a subway. It is odd, but we have got used to it.

Both the male and female teachers are counselling students when I walk in. The girl with the orange nail paint is waiting for an audience with the male teacher. I stare at her; a little envious that she has chosen to bypass the female teacher, even though I have done the same thing two days previously.

When the meditator has risen from her place at the female teacher's feet, I sit down on her cushion. The teacher turns to me kindly, with a benevolent smile. I know I have a tired expression on my face. I share the fact of the terrible pain on the right side of my forehead with her. I tell her I expect body pain and do not question it, but I cannot understand this chord of pain in my forehead. The teacher asks me if I move my eyes while meditating. As I reflect on this, I realize I do. My closed eyes seem to explore in tandem with my mind; 'seeing' all the parts I examine. The teacher advises me to stop moving my eyes during meditation. I rise from the cushion.

I am back in my room. There is a baby lizard on the mosquito net. *I have had enough of lizards and ticks and grasshoppers and meditation.* I want to go home. I am tired of the loneliness and the constant pain and the confusion regarding meditation as well as the lack of progress. I reach for my precious handkerchief; the one which has seen many tears now. I squeamishly reach out and wrap it around the lizard's body as I did with the grasshopper and throw it out with a swift movement.

I am totally worn out now with the effort of the past two days and no 'white light' or book. I force myself to wash up and eat dinner. Then I lie down in bed, exhausted beyond belief.

The same old thoughts surface: of nostalgia, of regret, of pain, of bitterness and of loss. I know I cannot force sleep, so I allow my mind to wander. They drift to old scars, which still bleed when prodded. I try and taste the familiar taste of bitterness upon my tongue. Surprisingly, today, it is less than what it used to be. Maybe I am ready to close old wounds. The knowledge does not surprise me. I have been through so much here. Quietly, I let the ghosts of the past rise up from my soul and drift away like formless vapour. Tonight, I can forgive completely. I forgive those who have hurt me and trespassed upon my soul and I tell their invisible forms, they are free.

My mind now starts calculating days once more. There is a part of me which wants to go back; anything would be easy compared to what I am going through here and I feel now that I will be able to handle my life. But now there is also that part of me which will forever be disjoint from that world.

I get up from bed to drink some water. As I look out onto the courtyard, I see the sevika coming in. It is nearly half past ten. It seems she sleeps late and wakes up very early. She locks the door of the courtyard. I am very surprised. I did not know we are locked in each night. The thought is both comforting and disturbing. Comforting because it makes me feel secure and disturbing, because I feel like a cloistered nun, destined to be here forever. There are only four more days to go, but it seems like an eternity.

8

SELF-DEFEAT

Day Seven

I WAKE UP LATE AGAIN BUT I DON'T CARE OVERMUCH NOW. It means less meditation time and less pain. I am surprised I should feel this way after Guruji has said every moment is precious. The sevika has not bothered to wake me up. She has probably been chastised enough.

I am fifteen minutes late. Once again, there are many empty seats in the hall. Many meditators are not coming for morning meditation anymore.

Everything seems to be going wrong today. My knee pain is so acute that I can hardly sit down. The forehead pain seems to have intensified during the night. And my back is beyond description. I no longer even try and sit straight. I do not last even twenty minutes in the cross-legged position. Moving, as usual, does not help. My right knee rebels against being folded to the side of my body. I try many different positions in the course of two hours. The rain yesterday has brought infections to the ashram and there are many people hacking and coughing and sneezing. The sounds jar in the silence. I cannot wait for the sitting to get over. When the eagerly awaited loud click of the player breaks the silence and the words 'anicca, anicca' are spoken, I hurriedly unfold my legs and bend them at the knees with the ankles touching my cushion. I wait for Guruji to conclude, but he is reciting a doha. I have opened my eyes. The others are still deep in meditation. Even though it costs me the last bit of effort to do so, I get into position again, though I do not close my eyes. Guruji said last night that when we see others erect like little Buddhas, we will feel self-doubt and craving. In spite of knowing this, that is exactly how I feel.

As my eyes go to the platform, I see that the female teacher is bent over with her chin almost on her bosom. I stare in amazement: a teacher not all erect and perfect? Everything is so confusing; especially, the technique. I am examining my back in horizontal lines, but I do not know if this is the correct way. Also, I have not been able to feel my backbone at all. The stomach is slightly easier now, because a self-propelled energy flow gently moves over its fleshy contours like a rolling wave. It is also strange and confusing how it takes me so long to pick out the faintest tingle on my head, whereas with my legs, I do not even have to try. As soon as my mind moves downwards from my torso, there is that flash of energy which moves from my hips, over my thighs and into my legs in one swift movement. In my arms, however, there is no such spontaneous flow.

I do not realize I am behaving contrary to the teachings of Dhamma, seeking what is not there.

I wait for the audiotape to end. I have never noticed before that Guruji's 'anicca' does not signal the end of a meditation session. It lasts a further five minutes after it. Five minutes can seem like an eternity when one is in such acute pain. I just about stop myself from getting up and moving out of the hall.

Finally, we are able to leave for breakfast. After I have finished breakfast, I linger in front of the notice board. Today, it has some beautiful Dhamma quotes. The female meditator who had volunteered information about her notepad and pen at the beginning of the course and promised not to use them, is busy copying them down. I feel infuriated at the audacity. I have had to steal pen and paper, write my notes secretly and then destroy them for meditation and here is a meditator who has no qualms about writing openly! I walk away in disgust.

I decide I will not carry dinner to my room from today. It has not done much for me and the initial excitement and hope that it will benefit me has gone. When I walk in to the courtyard, I realize it has not been swept for days. The little bit of rubbish I swept out of my room is still in a corner. I do not care anymore. There are only four more days to go and then all this will not matter.

I prepare to bathe. Baths at seven in the morning are de rigueur now. I walk unclothed into the bathroom and watch myself in the mirror. Several new red blotches have appeared on my abdomen. I gaze at the body which I have always looked at critically. In the small mirror, I can only see the small breasts, the extra flesh on the stomach and the fleshy thighs. Today, I do not cringe at the sight of imperfections. I accept my body for the way it looks and I am already comfortable with the roll of fat on my stomach. It is so important that we all accept ourselves the way we are, with all our imperfections and idiosyncrasies. It would make for a much more peaceful world if we did not constantly hanker after perfection and standardization.

I am bothered about the blotches though, and I glance in the corner of the bathroom towards where I had seen the ticks. Sure enough, there are several there, moving about in languid stupour. I cringe. My suspicion that these creatures crawl into my bed at night fills me with a sudden and inexplicable rage and I break another very important precept of Dhamma: I pick up my slipper and whack them to death. I feel like I have committed manslaughter just seconds after I am done. I look away in horror and quickly bathe and flush them down the drain with the bath water.

I have broken two important precepts I never thought I would: not to steal and not to kill. I am the same person who has lifted lizards and grasshoppers and put them out. The same girl who felt terrible when a crow flew away with a lizard; the same person who pushes beetles and bugs out of the way when they come too close in the discourse hall. I fear what I have done will interfere with my meditation and feel all hope is lost for me.

There is a peacock atop the pagoda today. The bells on the spire are tinkling and I am filled with a longing I cannot define. I walk on towards the meditation hall. There, in the grass on the side are three grass-cutters. Men in this part of the ashram where I have seen only women for the past seven days! I am suddenly dumbstruck as to what to do. I feel naked and exposed even though I am on the triangular walkway. I quickly turn and walk away.

My body feels heavier now because my period has started and I am more languid today than in the past seven days. As I walk back, I encounter the old sevika. Impulsively, I stop her and ask her what day it is and when the course will be ending. She does not seem too taken aback and answers that we have four more days to go and we will leave on the twenty-ninth. How four more days add up to the twenty-ninth is something I still cannot figure out.

I sit down on the raised edge of the path. Four more days. I do not know if I am up to the challenge. Maybe I have already achieved what I came here to do. I have reconciled my faith and my new found strength and I have forgiven those who have harmed and hurt me. What more can I possibly want? But, deep down, I know I crave for freedom from melancholy, the biggest bane of my existence on earth. There has never been a time when I have truly been happy. I must somehow fit in with the only acceptable societal norm of pragmatism and nonchalance and not dwell too deep in pain ever again.

I can already feel my body revolting against the torture it is going to be put through. I tremble slightly. I head towards the meditation hall with a heavy heart. The American is walking in front of me and she swings her steel water bottle as she ambles along in her distinct gait. I wonder how the others are faring. I cannot see any visible signs of discomfort on anyone. The old lady with the gold nose studs looks very sad, but that is perhaps because she also has some old pain, which she has not been able to reconcile with.

I notice a woman walking towards the hall in low-heeled sandals. She makes a clattering sound as she walks. She also has *payals* or anklets on her feet and is dressed in a gaudy salwar kameez. It seems she has just arrived here, for I do not know of anyone else who can walk in heels after so many days of debilitating pain.

I am very irritable today. When I sit down upon my cushion in the hall, I smell strong jasmine hair oil and I silently curse the woman who has applied it to her hair. It is nauseating in this closed atmosphere and is hugely distracting. I am also angry at the peacocks who sit atop the roof of the hall. Their loud calls are getting to be more and more disturbing and seem to pierce into my skin.

I know we are not supposed to chant or use any imagery in our minds while meditating, but all knowledge and wisdom seems to have evaporated into thin air at this stage. Unable to cope with the pain that fires up straight away, I start reciting the *Hanuman Chalisa*. The prayer is supposed to ward away evil and give strength. When all else fails, I still surrender to God. As I chant silently, I find it easier to block out the immense pain. I chant the prayer throughout the sitting.

Of course, I am a failure. When the break is announced, I head out quickly and start stretching my body, trying to shake off the pain. Surprisingly, the American is doing the same and I realize now that everyone else is also going through the same kind of hardship. I bend sideways and forward and stretch my legs out forward and backward. This course feels like it is over for me. I have no clue what this meditation is achieving, even if bits of it have been wondrous and amazing. I will soon be back to where I started from.

During the next sitting, I chant my prayer again. My body has involuntarily started rocking back and forth with the pain. The movement helps disburse it a little, but I know it must look extremely strange to anyone watching. When the male teacher announces group checking, I am relieved for the little recess it will provide and wait eagerly to be called up. The teacher admonishes a girl in our group for talking in the rooms during meditation hours. This is the first rebuke I hear in the ashram.

Many irrelevant and silly questions are put forth and most of the replies are unsatisfactory. I try to glean some nuggets of wisdom or helpful tips, but learn nothing that could help me understand the technique better or clear my doubts and confusion. Soon after, it is announced that we may leave the hall and go to the pagoda.

I am frightened when I open the door to my cell because of the absence of other meditators, the missing comforting gaze or mere presence of the teachers and the stark contrast to the openness of the meditation hall. I place my satchel and bottle to a side, unclasp the hook of my trousers to get more comfortable and then unhook the clasp of my bra as well. I sit atop the little cushion which rests on the bigger one but it is no longer comfortable to sit this way. I place it to a side and sit on the edge of the big cushion with my legs in cross-legged position upon the floor. I have to face the truth that there is no running away from the pain. I close my eyes and start concentrating.

My body is already covered in beads of sweat. I press

along; taking solace from the fact that this causes a tickling, wet and cool sensation. An energy flow cascades slowly down my back and torso. This does not feel like a remarkable occurrence. I am only focused on being able to sit motionless for an hour. Along with the spontaneous energy flows, there is the horrifying pain. I have unshed tears behind my eyes; tears of supreme effort, tears of feeling like a failure, tears of regret and tears for my book. My brain is screaming silently. The pain has risen to a crescendo which has caused rivulets of sweat to run down my body. Even through flashes of pure agony which remind me of the pain of childbirth, I do not get up, though I shift position once. When the bell rings, it is unexpected, because I have lost track of time. Sobs rack my body instantly. I have spent a complete hour in the cell. But it is surely an effort I will not ever be able to replicate again.

Slowly and with tears still wet upon my face and my body trembling with tiredness, I make my way out of the pagoda. The first touch of air upon my face is heaven after the furnace-like heat of the cell. I am so drained that I cannot walk more than a few steps. I sit down on the edge of the path near the pagoda and mull over my experience. I shake my head in wonder and disbelief. I have experienced the same level of pain at childbirth, but I do not know why we are constantly self-flagellating ourselves.

I want to forget everything. I go to my room and draw the curtain. The room is considerably cooler. I lie down on the hard bed and try to force the pain out of my body. The disillusionment washes over me in relentless waves. The tiny room, the narrow, uncomfortable bed, the stone slabs, the coarse blanket, the silence, the iron doors of the courtyard, the rubbish left ungathered; all of it is getting to me. This place has begun to feel like a prison. I miss my daughter immensely and cannot shake of a morbid feeling that I will never see her again. I wonder what she is doing just now and this makes me ache even more. My eyes, moist with pain, close with tiredness and I fall off to sleep. However, my brain is so attuned to timings that I wake up at half past twelve.

Outside my block, the woman with the anklets and heeled sandals is talking to the grumpy sevika. She looks even sadder and I overhear a few words without meaning to. She is talking about her son and saying something about a phone call. Though I walk away as quickly as I can, I feel an instant and acute empathy with the woman. She is probably missing her child just the way I am and could not resist the urge to share her grief.

It is from this day onwards that I will notice the women starting to gravitate towards each other, ignoring rules. They will walk in pairs and congregate in groups. The only ones who will adhere to rules till the end are the American, the Italian, A, the girl in flared pants, the girl with orange nail paint and I.

As we walk towards the hall, I see smoke emanating from near the water cooler. There are two men near it, trying to smoke away the wasps, which have congregated there in hordes today because of the heat. I am not frightened of them because I am in the midst of a group of women. I am glad the wasps are being smoked out and not otherwise harmed.

In the hall, room keys jangle loudly in the silence. My senses are so sharp that every sound resonates with twice its normal force. I wish the keys would be placed down gently. The overpowering smell of jasmine hair oil and the heat make my head spin. I almost weep inside with frustration. Any distraction at this stage magnifies the pain.

I have started rocking my body back and forth constantly during meditation. The wide, comfortable cushion, which I so appreciated on the first day, now feels like the most uncomfortable perch in the world. As for the smaller cushion, no one sits atop it anymore.

I move many times in one sitting, quite a regression from yesterday and also from the hour spent in the pagoda. It is not only the extreme pain which is making me restless and agitated today; it is also the fact that I am simply too bored. We have been practising vipassanā for more than ten hours a day for four days now and there is no longer any novelty regarding the technique.

The boredom worries me. I can tolerate the pain, but what do I do about the boredom? My mind is now freer to think because the energy flows are spontaneous in many parts; but lesser concentration produces more discomfort.

All around me are huge sighs, as if souls, caged too long, are being set free. The coughing continues, sometimes incessantly, from the person afflicted. I keep waiting for the person to leave of his own accord or be told to do so, but it never happens. I think about my book and how I sacrificed it for a greater goal. But the greater goal is nowhere in sight.

In the break, I exercise again, willing some of the joints to loosen up. These few moments are precious if I am to last another two hours. Except for the American, everyone else is sitting around, too tired to even stand. Their heads are down and I can sense the exhaustion and dejection.

No one sits in the cross-legged pose anymore. Everyone has at least one leg at an awkward angle. The American's hands are no longer bravely on her knees. They are placed languidly in her lap. The Italian is obviously in considerable pain too. I relish these sights, though it does not take away from my own sense of failure. I look at the male meditators. Strangely, the bespectacled man is sitting without any apparent discomfort. But the meditator who really astonishes me is one right in front. He is sitting perfectly erect and his body looks relaxed. I fancy I can almost see his calm expression.

My eyes move towards the women in the front rows. I have never extended the boundary of my observation beyond the

Italian and American. The Punjabi is calmly sitting cross-legged. The little cushion is in her lap and her hands are on top of it. The girl from the mother-daughter duo is also sitting in the same fashion and even has her hands on her knees! My mouth falls open.

All the wisdom about observing only one's own reality disappears, leaving behind a deep sense of dejection and failure. I am the only one who has her eyes open. I turn around and glance at the clock. There is a lot of time left for the sitting to get over. With a deep sigh, I tuck my legs in and close my eyes.

I cannot stop my eyes from moving in tandem with my mind and it feels like they are constantly out of their sockets. My face is contorted, but I cannot change its expression. I am very worried. I had stopped paying attention to Guruji's instructions in the last two days because they were getting increasingly repetitive and monotonous, but now realize to my dismay that I have missed some instructions about penetrating the skin and feeling sensations below it. How will I now be able to accomplish this?

I start observing my breath to calm my mind. Guruji has said it is acceptable to do this when we feel agitated. It does not help because I know no break or discourse or ending of the day is going to give me any further succour.

As I gaze at the Aravalis at tea time, the world outside seems like a chimera. I feel like a lost and forgotten soul and if I never go back, I doubt life would stop for anyone. I feel unwanted and alienated. My voice is gone and even if I could share my angst with anyone, I doubt the words would come. The silence has gone in too deep. There is a world full of hustle and bustle and relationships outside, but it is a world which I do not know anymore; a world to which I do not belong.

The same peacock is on the same tree, on the same perch, at the same time. Everything has acquired an element of jadedness about it; a sense of déjà vu; a sense of stillness and endless perpetuity.

I move out of my room about twenty minutes before the bell. I am too tired to walk, so I sit on the parapet on the edge of the walkway and gaze at the pagoda. What eagerness and enthusiasm I had for this evocative structure when I came here. I could not even wait to enter its sacred and hallowed portals. Most of my illusions have long since evaporated into thin air.

In the evening session, Guruji repeats some instructions about piercing and penetrating, but I cannot understand them. Since I am obviously behind the rest now, I determine to at least sit still once again, despite all odds. When I try to do so, my pelvic joints start screaming in agony and the cobra in my back shoots forth its terrible venom as if to sway me from my determination. I observe the enormous physical pain with a deep sadness and regret for all the pain I have accumulated all these years. I let it overpower me, to atone for the choices which caused my suffering; and then the unexpected happens once again. No 'white light' flashes inside my body; no jolt either. But my body starts 'cooling down'. The cooling starts from my legs and then the pain oozes slowly out of almost every part of my body. Miraculously, the cobra in my back coils up after so many days of tormenting me and goes off to sleep as if tired.

I quietly savour the slow cooling down of my body, unable to react to anything anymore. It is good that I don't, because the state of painlessness does not last very long. Though the back pain has vanished with the dreaded cobra having gone off to sleep, the pelvic joints start revolting again. I am experiencing the living wisdom which Guruji spoke about and I do not know it. I have experienced the truth of impermanence and the value of equanimity, yet I do not feel victorious.

When I emerge from the meditation hall, I am terribly

grateful that my back does not hurt. The cobra is dead. I had grown so used to living with intolerable levels of pain that the absence of it in my back is a strange feeling. Still, the prospect of sitting without a backrest is not appealing and when I see the three cushions against the wall in the mini hall already occupied, I feel a sense of frustration and dejection.

As we wait for the television set to be switched on, I observe P, the girl with the orange nail paint. All the glamour and bravado of the first day is gone from her. I suppose it is the same for all of us. We have all been stripped of our façades and protective masks and are like newborns; helpless, innocent and in the need of a mentor. A big black beetle comes scurrying towards P at top speed. P is visibly startled. I reach out and flick it neatly to make it to go scurrying in the opposite direction. Unfortunately, it is overturned and now struggles to get upright by kicking out its hairy legs. P and I both watch with fascination. There is telepathy between us of compassion for the creature. The sanctity of life and living things, big and small, is a lesson which has been learnt well by all of us.

Even though each action here feels like a mammoth and gigantic task, I reach out and flick the poor creature again, thinking it will land properly on its feet this time. But the creature only lands in a different spot, still struggling against the ignominy and indignity imposed on it. With a sigh I lift it up and put it upright again. However, it comes determinedly towards P again. This time P takes her cue from me and sends it away a little more gently than me. P and I have communicated without words and I will always remember how strong a silent connect can be. We humans have weakened our extra sensory abilities and gained nothing in their place.

When the discourse starts and Guruji says there are three days left, I am back to feeling fearful. Three days is not enough time for the 'deep surgical operation of the mind' I have been waiting for. Guruji compounds the fear by saying there are actually only two more days, because the tenth day does not really count. I know from my friend that the vow of silence will be lifted on the tenth day. Guruji says that the noble silence will become noble 'chattering' on the tenth day. The audience laughs obligingly. Guruji says that there is nothing noble about chattering and that chattering and meditation do not go hand in hand; yet, the tenth day is very important because it would act like a shock absorber before we faced the world outside on the eleventh day. It would be a soothing balm to our wounds.

Guruji wipes his perspiring face and says that from here on, the Buddha wants us to meditate continuously, even in recess periods. I am incredulous. The recesses are necessary to recover, but Guruji is telling us that there should be no more of them. As if to demonstrate that this is not a big deal, he says people come here on courses which last twenty or thirty days without recess. Surely Guruji jests. But apparently, Guruji is serious. He says that for the next two days, we have to learn how to practice vipassanā continuously.

We are mostly aware of our actions; now we have to be aware of sensations as well. We must maintain continuity of awareness at least in our moving parts, such as the legs while walking. Even while resting and lying down, we can be aware of sensations. Guruji says students are sometimes unable to sleep well during a course. He says this is not a cause for worry, because the student would still wake up feeling rested if he or she observed sensations with equanimity. Nature designed sleep for two reasons. One was so that the body could rest and the other was to rest the mind. Lying down, the body does not use any energy for any activity and the observation of sensations gives the mind a rest from rapid and random thoughts. The camera suddenly wobbles in the hands of the cameraperson and Guruji gets a little lopsided. He nevertheless continues without a pause.

He says there are three states of mind: wakefulness, sleep and dreaming. A yogi is one who attains communion with the ultimate truth and exists in none of these states. The entire world sleeps, but a yogi remains awakened.

Guruji says after the seven days here, storms may accost us, but we will have the strength to face them. The five nīvaranas will still be there but there will also be five friends to help us. The first of these is *saddhā* or faith. But faith could not be blind faith. Each of these friends would have to be accompanied by wisdom.

He narrates an encounter with a woman from the Bhakti cult of India, who became a vipassanā meditator. Though her meditation was exemplary, she could not reconcile the teachings of vipassanā with her complete love, devotion and surrender towards God. She came to him anguished over the possibility of losing her devotion because of vipassanā. Guruji asked her what bhakti entailed and whether they made promissory offerings to God in the Bhakti cult. The woman said promissory offerings were a part of devotion and prayer. Guruji explained to her that blind devotion is meaningless. He gave the example of the Indian God Rama and how many people called themselves devotees of Rama but never imbibed his divine qualities.

Humans created God in their own image and believed Him to be as susceptible to flattery and promises as they themselves. Such a God, Guruji says, would be like a 'mad Goenka', obsessed with his name and wanting to see and hear it everywhere and wanting people to chant 'Hare Goenka, Hare Goenka.' This is hilarious for two reasons. Firstly, Guruji's family name is Goenka. His family has many schools and other institutions in their name. It quite sounds as if he is mocking his kinsmen. Secondly, while saying 'Hare Goenka', Guruji stretches his arms out wide and then brings them together to clap his hands loudly. Everyone laughs loudly.

Guruji says there are also devotees of Christ who are fanatical in their devotion towards the 'Son of God'; the most compassionate one, who forgave even those who put him onto the crucifix; but bear ill will and hatred in their hearts towards their fellow men. Christ needs no testimonial of devotion from His followers. Anyone who lives a life of truth, love and compassion is a Son of God. And so it was with all religions. Guruji says there are followers of Buddha who chant *Buddham Sharnam Gachhami* constantly; which means 'I take refuge in the Buddha'. He says it is meaningless to chant these words if one is a true follower of Buddha, because the Buddha only preached refuge in one's own enlightenment.

He laughs softly and says India has lost the meaning of the word Bhagwan or God. He says there are Bhagwans as numerous as the monsoon frogs. Everyone laughs again. Guruji says Bhagwan is one who has destroyed all *raaga* or craving and all *dvesha* or aversion and also all ignorance, illusion and delusion; an arahant who has killed all his enemies. Guruji asks who one's enemies are and says they are the defilements within. The one who has killed all mental defilements and has no trace of impurities in his mind is an arahant. We have to work towards our salvation ourselves.

If one becomes perfect in theory and in practice, Guruji says, one will have the qualities of Buddha, who practised what he preached and preached what he practised. That is why he was called the tathāgata, or the one who had walked on the path of personal experience of the truth. The Buddha attained enlightenment at the age of thirty-five and spent the next forty-five years serving others, teaching them Dhamma with infinite love and compassion.

Three months prior to his death at the age of eighty, the Buddha reached a place called Kushinagar in the eastern part of India, attended by a follower named Ananda. On the night he passed away, he lay under a tree with the full moon overhead. Ananda decided to inform people about the Buddha's presence in the city and the fact that he would soon be gone from them.

Hordes of people queued up to pay their last respects to Buddha. One follower would not budge and let the queue proceed. He insisted that he needed to learn Dhamma from the Buddha. Ananda was shocked and said this was not the time for anyone to learn Dhamma. But the Buddha heard the pleas of the man and asked for him to be brought forward. Then, with his last few breaths, he imparted his teaching to the man he believed was desperately in need of it.

Dhamma's benefits, Guruji says, do not accrue in the future; they are not like post-dated cheques for a bank above the clouds. Loud laughter follows. In Dhamma, there was no gap between actions and rewards.

The discourse is over. I glance at the clock. The discourse has lasted more than an hour.

I need to speak to the male teacher. I need to be explained where all this is leading. In the break, I stand determinedly before him. The teacher smiles and nods for me to sit. My voice is clearer today. I start by telling him that I have surrendered my book as he advised me to. He nods his head with a smile. I tell him that the sixth day did not go off as badly as was forewarned and expected. Again, he nods with a smile, perhaps happy that I seem to have no complaints today. But my next statement shakes him out of complacency. I ask him what the purpose of all this self-flagellation is and why we are undergoing this seemingly purposeless torture.

I have started equating the technique of vipassanā with the self-infliction of pain followed in some sects. He is visibly taken aback at my choice of words and contradicts me immediately. He says the purpose of vipassanā is not to inflict torture at all and I must not think of it in terms of self-flagellation. But he also fails to explain exactly why we are enduring the terrible and endless pain and fails to ease my feeling of persecution. I come away no more comforted than before. I blush at the admonishment I have received. I had great expectations of being the ideal meditator.

I can barely sit for the twenty minutes left for the day to end, when the bell rings out softly. It is a slow, sad walk back to the residential block. The tears are very close but I hold them back. I want to do as Guruji says, but I no longer know where I am going. I have surrendered my book for a purpose which is now lost to me.

I look up at the star-studded sky and I see lights of aeroplanes high above near the horizon. I also see something else. I see the loose pages of my unwritten book flying in the wind. It is finally all over, like an unfulfilled promise of love; a memory which will eventually be lost to time. I only manage to hold back the tears till I reach my room and then lean against the door and cry.

9

THE POWER OF ACCEPTANCE

❦

Day Eight

I WAKE UP DEJECTED. IT HAS RAINED ONCE AGAIN DURING the night. I carry my pillowcase with me. I shine my torch glumly in front of me on the path and hang my umbrella on the rack outside the meditation hall. We all look like a bunch of woebegone ghosts in the silvery darkness. There are again many empty seats in the meditation hall. By now I know that they belong to those who have deliberately chosen to stay away in the non-adhishtan sittings. Many are just biding their time until the completion of the course. I sit down with a feeling of ennui and vacuity. I have lost my determination and in a way, I am also biding my time till the end of the course. If the male teacher had given me some satisfactory answers, I might have found the courage and renewed strength to carry on.

I am puzzled about my backbone. It is still a blind region. When I examine my back horizontally, I try to 'move' the energy over it and feel its hardness, but there is nothing; it is as if it does not exist. It is the same when I move down vertically; I can feel most of my back, but the backbone just refuses to come alive. But my nether region has developed constant pulsation. I should have clarified these doubts with the teacher. I will have to go to him once again. The American does so nearly every day and so does P. I have not yet heard any rebuke against this, though not one male meditator has approached the female teacher so far. I smile inside at the thought of a male meditator in conversation with our conservative female teacher.

The pain in my hips has overrun the pain in the back, which, till yesterday, threatened to suffocate the very breath out of me with its power. I am finding it extremely difficult to sit with the pain in my joints; it is a dreadful pain I have never experienced before. The other reason is an embarrassing one: I need to use the toilet. The urge is huge and I contemplate leaving the hall. The idea of being out of the hall and in my room is hugely tempting. I can even go off to sleep. Only the embarrassment at being seen walking out and Guruji's words of working seriously even in recess keeps me from doing so.

I start meditating again, trying to lose myself in the highly intense and onerous task. I start from the top of my head and start making my way downwards. I tell myself if I cannot suppress the urge, I will leave the hall. A strange thing happens. After about twenty minutes, the urge has completely disappeared. I am stupefied at this, but assume once again that intense concentration yields strange and amazing results. I am glad I did not miss a session of meditation after all.

Guruji's doha recital begins at six in the meditation hall. I listen to the words today. Today's doha is about the night of darkness getting over and the breaking of dawn. It sends a chill down my spine, bringing forth hope for deliverance but also the fear that it shall not happen. The dawn may break, but there is no break in the pain; only a greater and more fierce yearning for release. The singing goes on till half past six and today I realize the heaviness of each single minute of that half hour. When the singing starts fading away, I am trembling with the effort of holding on.

While walking slowly down the path to the dining hall, I remember Guruji's words about not taking a break in meditation even during recess. He has advised feeling sensations associated with activity and I focus my attention on my legs while walking. I am surprised to feel feeble currents running down in them. So my mind is sharp enough now to feel vibrations even without sitting down to meditate. It is remarkable that an ordinary person cannot feel any such sensations, but after eight days of training, they become spontaneous. It makes me think that there may be so many obvious truths within which we may be missing because of our minds not being sharp enough. This would have made for an interesting read in my book, but my book no longer exists. Its pages flew away in the wind last night and must now be scattered all over the low hills – dirty, wet and torn.

Guruji's singing has recommenced. It intensifies my loneliness and fragility.

As I sit on my chair in the dining hall with my meal on the steel tabletop, I once again remember Guruji's words. No recess. We must feel the sensations connected with each activity. I am sipping some hot, sweet milk. My hands are cupping the little steel glass. I feel a tiny tremble in my fingers and the smooth, warm surface of the metal. I bring the glass closer to my lips and note the muscle movements associated with the action. When I place the rim of the glass on my lips, I register the tremble of my mouth. I take a sip of the milk. Its flavour is deeper than I have ever tasted before. And I realize another thing. Milk is salty. Yes, it has a salty, metallic taste.

From here on, I will constantly be in touch with sensations associated with every activity, big and small. Tastes and smell will be amplified and enhanced upon my tongue and nose.

I will feel sounds in the form of vibrations entering my ears and walking will never be the spontaneous activity again. It is a whole new world I have entered, with little space for idle thought. I am truly within my being now.

Even as I wash my utensils, I feel the touch of water upon my hands and the greasy feel of soap. It is not merely external stimuli that I register now; it is also the pulsating vibrations under the skin. My body feels truly alive.

I stop outside the dining hall to read the notices. There is nothing new or of any import today. All the notices end with the words 'bhavatu sabba managalam' and 'be happy'. The 'be happy' is decorated with little flowers and one could almost be led to believe all is well here in the ashram and proceeding as per plan: deep surgical operations have been performed and defilements have come out. And I am ready to head back to the world and life outside – a new, rejuvenated, reborn me.

I read the notice again about the stipulated time for question hour with the teachers and suddenly feel I have lost out on much time and wisdom by not utilizing these slots, when the teachers have been available to dedicatedly tend to the students.

There is also the thought for the day: 'The deeper the craving, the deeper is the aversion and the deeper the aversion, the deeper is the affliction.' I understand this intellectually but I will only be able to experientially grasp its meaning many months afterwards.

I am alone as I walk back towards the triangular walkway. On the path, I spot a fat green caterpillar. It will surely be trampled upon. Love and compassion flowing from my being, I unfold the pillowcase over it and lift it up. Then, I gently fling it upon the long tufts of grass on the side and hope that a peacock is not on the lookout for a tasty meal.

It is time to wash my clothes again. The cold water stings, but I am used to it now. Guruji has spoken often about the glow that meditators' faces acquire because of vipassanā, but I do not see it on my face. I look at myself in the mirror. Having been in close contact with all colours, shapes and sizes for the past few days and having seen virtually 'under' my skin; skin that is one-sixteenth of an inch deep, has made me realize even more the worthlessness of outward appearance and the value of character over appearance. I do not see myself as a woman but a human being who has been given this particular body to house the mind and soul. The flaws have just ceased to matter.

A few ticks still lurk in their favourite corner and I turn my face away. Another three days and all this will be over; for good or for bad. I bathe, dress and hang out my washing. As usual, I am early and I step out to stroll. I walk almost up to the dining hall, passing the female teacher's quarters on the way. There is no one else about. Apparently, the strain is telling on the teachers, too. The female teacher is scolding someone loudly and harshly and I assume, for some reason, that it is her daughter she is castigating. She does not seem to be bothered about listening ears. I am embarrassed and I quickly turn back onto the triangular walkway.

The mother-daughter duo has apparently given up their efforts for a bit. I once again feel a deep sense of loneliness: a loneliness I fear will not go away even after I leave here. I tap my umbrella forlornly on the ground in case there are any monkeys in the vicinity, but it seems like everyone has fled the ashram and I am the only soul left here.

Women meditators now walk in pairs or groups, oblivious to rules. They now also speak audibly, uncaring even of the teacher, whose quarters are close by. A few of them even sit together on the edge of the walkway, bunched together. I wonder what is going on. A woman walks out of the residential block with a tumbler around which a sacred red thread is tied. Guruji's advice about shunning rituals here seems to have gone unheeded. Another woman is sitting on the parapet and practising *pranayama* (yogic breathing exercises); in spite of having been told of the dangers of mixing other techniques with the technique of vipassanā. It is as if everything is unravelling and people are fast going back to the way of life they knew before coming here. I shake my head in disbelief and start walking towards the meditation hall to get away from all the insanity.

Everyone is reluctant to meditate. The American, like me, is stretching out her legs and flexing them constantly at the knee. The Italian is slumped over and her poise seems to have disintegrated. The girl in flared pants is slumped and downcast. I am glad to know I am not alone in my misery. There is nothing more heartening than to see others undergoing the same hardship.

Guruji's instructions now are to 'sweep' the body with a free flow wherever possible and examine the rest of the parts separately. As always, he urges us to maintain equanimity. Sitting sideways, I start meditating but I remain conscious of little else but pain and boredom.

Guruji ends the first sitting of the afternoon with an exceedingly long 'bhavatu sabba managalam'. Our bodies must all collectively be screaming with pain, waiting to chant 'sadhu', and get over with the ordeal. A thought occurs to me that a wise and smiling Guruji might be testing the limits of our endurance: pushing us to the brink and seeing who falls off the edge.

In the next session, for the first time, I feel a little sleepy. I know it is sheer ennui and a sense of defeat that is causing the stupour. My mind, getting accustomed to feeling free energy flows, is free to think despondent thoughts.

I choose the meditation cell once again. I notice from the footwear that the American, the Italian, P and the girl in flared pants have all chosen to still meditate in the pagoda. So I am not the most resilient and determined of the lot. It adds further to the sense of failure.

My spirits sink in the cell today. I have sat for barely twenty minutes on the cushion to meditate when I suddenly give up my efforts. I stand up and leave the cell. It is more than a sense of defeat; it is a huge sense of resignation towards my inability to carry on.

I walk towards the residential block without looking back at the pagoda or the meditation hall. Many of my soul sisters are still in the pagoda, hanging on with grit. I don't envy them anymore: the girls sitting straight-backed in the hall; the ones in the pagoda. May the best fruits accrue to those who deserve them.

There is still half an hour left. Though I have planned to sleep till lunch, the strength and resilience I have acquired in the past seven days keeps me from giving up completely. Instead of lying down to sleep, I sit up in bed and start meditating. There are two or three women in the block who are going about their chores at this time. Sounds of sweeping and talking assault my brain, but I am at a stage where this does not frazzle or annoy me.

The pain hammers away at me like a sledgehammer on an anvil, but I keep concentrating, while my body gets drenched with sweat. Things can get no worse; my mind seems to be telling itself. There will be no comfort for me if I move. If I give up now, I will only have to go back to the task at a later stage. The pain will not go. With this silent soliloquy, I continue moving down and up, searching and feeling my mind. The pain might kill me today, I tell myself, but there is no point living with defeat anyway. As soon as this thought comes to my mind, suddenly and abruptly, the pain in my left hip joint and leg disappears, leaving a kind of nothingness in its wake.

The gong for lunch goes off at almost the same time, but I do not open my eyes. Once again, copious tears run down my face and fall on my bed. Painlessness in any part of the body at this stage is unimaginable succour and I savour it even though I know I can get up and leave for lunch. I finally open my eyes when it is fifteen past eleven. I rise slowly. There is no one about. I head quickly for lunch. On the way, I meet the young sevika who is rushing up the path towards me. She admonishes me, saying we all must be present in the dining hall at the prescribed time. I am mortified and annoyed: mortified that I have been castigated, and annoyed that my supreme effort has been undermined. But my voice is somewhere deep within my soul and I simply nod my head dumbly at her.

I eat very little now. It is as if I eat just for sustenance: always a cherished goal. I wonder why I have been admonished as I still finish faster than most meditators who are still enjoying their meals. My washed clothes are half dry upon the clothesline and I pull them further out to catch the sun. I hurry back up the path because I want to be in the meditation hall at twelve with the teachers.

I am not the only one in the throes of doubt. There are several meditators in the hall. I see the American and P with the male teacher. Feeling left out, I see no reason why three should be a crowd. This question hour seems to be more informal than the brief meetings with the teachers in between meditation sessions. I grab my little cushion and walking up quickly to the platform, hurriedly sit down at the male teacher's feet without waiting for permission. Obviously, I have to let the American and P speak before me. I am so lost in framing the questions that I do not really hear what the American says. It is the same with P. I do notice that P has a very strong American accent.

It is my turn. I fumble with words even as I try hard to sound articulate. The formidable environment, the authority of the teachers and the noble silence of so many days has made clear and crisp expression a thing of the past. After a couple of sentences, however, my voice becomes stronger. I no longer touch upon the subject of endless self-infliction of pain. I have already shocked the male teacher once by mentioning self-flagellation. Instead, I ask him how I should go about 'feeling' my back and backbone. The teacher answers that it is not necessary to feel the backbone. It is, once again, an unsatisfactory answer and puzzles me because I expect this nerve-centre to be fuller of sensations than any other part of the body. When I ask about other blind areas, he gesticulates to give me the analogy of a torchlight beam, which lights up an area briefly and then is gone.

It seems I will never get any satisfactory replies here, but I thank the teacher and move away. As I am about to go out of the hall, the female teacher, unoccupied for the moment, smiles and beckons for me to come up. I sit at her feet on one of the cushions placed there. She asks me in a very kind voice how my meditation is going and I struggle to fight back tears. I tell her I have regressed and cannot sit even for twenty minutes in the cross-legged position anymore. The female teacher is in a happy and talkative mood today. Or maybe she just likes me. Whatever it is, she tells me it is difficult even for *her* to sit cross-legged for a full hour. My eyes widen in amazement. It is true that I have often seen her slumped over during adhishtan, with her head almost on her chest. But I always thought the teachers were invincible. The teacher further tells me that she has to unfold her legs in the last five or ten minutes of a sitting. This knowledge is truly amazing and comforting. If the teacher cannot do adhishtan for an hour, who am I to be able to aspire to it? I have a sneaky suspicion, however, that she may not be as qualified as her male counterpart, who is definitely, and I refuse to believe otherwise; invincible. He sits calmly and erect during adhishtan, without any hint of strain. Still, the female teacher's words have a soothing effect on me.

What she tells me next acts as a lifeline for my last three days at the ashram. She says when the pain gets unbearable, I can lift my thighs from the ground without opening out my legs and changing position. She shows me how to do it. I have this incredible urge to hug her, but a slight smoothening of the furrows on my forehead and a glint of hope in my eyes is probably all the reward she needs. I thank her and move out of the hall. Back in my room, I slump on the bed and will myself to sleep. For once, I am able to and I rouse myself just before the bell.

After my talk with the teachers, I am calmer, though the sadness is still there. There have been no life-altering revelations till now and I have no reason to believe that the remaining two days will do anything for me.

I force myself into the cross-legged pose. I have tried many tricks and ways to hold on during adhishtan: chanting of prayers, rocking my body back and forth and sitting sideways. Now I am going to give it one final try with the slight lifting of my thighs as demonstrated by the female teacher.

The pain is worst in my hip joints. The venom of the cobra is almost a memory and though I allude this to the law of impermanence, I have yet to be able to subscribe to it in entirety. I have experienced terrible pain in the legs and back come and go, but I still view my physical hardships as a permanent feature.

I now lift up my thighs every ten minutes or so. This does indeed give temporary relief without me having to thrash about and change position. I quietly concentrate on flows in the body. Gone are the pin pricks and feather touches. The sensations in my body are now currents as swift as tides, especially in my legs, even though they are numb.

The pain is too severe for me to survive its onslaught merely by the lifting of thighs and I soon shift sideways. Soon it will be time for adhishtan. In the short break after the first hour, I again exercise my body. I am standing in a bit of shade near the bathrooms, where there is more foliage. A little distance away, the American is also stretching like me. Then the hand bell tinkles and we head back in.

Adhishtan. I manage to sit cross-legged for forty minutes just by lifting my thighs periodically and it is a tremendous achievement, even though I feel I am cheating. When the familiar strains of 'anicca, anicca' are spoken and the doha has been recited, I open my eyes to an overcast sky. There is also a chill in the air. My spirits lift, much like that of a peacock sensing rain. It has been a terribly warm day.

I head out gladly under the breezy, dark sky and look around with pleasure at a changed world. However, the gladness is short lived, for all of a sudden, it starts to rain in torrents. My first thought is of my washed clothes, almost dry, on the line. My precious full-sleeved tee is there and I will need it tomorrow morning. I see a short-haired girl running towards the residential block and hope that she will take everyone's washing off the line. I cannot even imagine myself walking fast, let alone running to the block.

Most of us scramble inside the meditation hall, where it is now stuffy compared to outside. A few meditators stay back on the steps of the hall, enjoying the lashing rain. One of the girls who I have noticed before and whose appearance and behaviour are like those of a coy film actress, takes off her slippers and runs out into the rain with abandon. She hops around and squeals with her face upturned to the sky. I am shocked at the wanton behaviour. No one rebukes her. In fact, the young sevika stands on the steps and laughs at the spectacle. Youth is, I muse, exuberant, resilient and hedonistic.

I realize I am a bit envious.

My calves are wet and I use my handkerchief to wipe them. I shake my head at the behaviour of the girl and wonder what is happening to all the sanctity and silence of the first few days. Soon, we are all back in our places and silence descends in the hall. The meditation begins, with a sudden spate of sneezing and hacking and I roll my eyes behind closed lids. I have learnt to continue to meditate with several distractions of sound and smell, but I am still aware of them. I sit in the cross-legged position, lifting my thighs whenever the pain gets unbearable. All of a sudden, there is a cascade in my upper body: it is like a bucket of cold water being emptied slowly over me. I start shivering, but the cascade does not stop. Unfortunately, it stops at the pelvic girdle, where the rings of pain begin.

Guruji has spoken about this kind of waterfall effect and it is a beautiful and amazing experience. But he has also warned us against the pitfalls of clinging to cravings and pleasant sensations. I enjoy the cascade, but tell myself that it is temporary and that it will pass. I must not expect this to be a regular phenomenon. The threshold of pain was crossed, a 'white light' came and went, a huge and powerful cobra went off to sleep, the fire of agony cooled down when least expected and now I am experiencing the cascade. It is all maya, I tell myself; it is all illusion. Guruji is right. It is all anicca.

Just before the break at four, I am unable to continue meditating and I open my eyes to look at the clock on the wall at the back. I spy P just behind me. I have never looked at the meditators behind me, so I did not know that only a narrow aisle separates us. P's body is all askew. Her long and thin legs are stretched out on the side and her back is bent. The American and Italian are faring no better. They are in obvious discomfort and their legs are outstretched too. I am comforted by the sight.

As I head out of the hall in the break, I see P has not stood up from her seat. She has her head between her knees and I suddenly feel sorry for her. The rain has stopped and everything is wet and green. I expect to see several peacocks with their beautiful tails spread out after the rain, but I can only hear their calls. I stand near the water cooler and admire the scene. Just then, the female teacher emerges from the meditation hall and heads towards the path. As she crosses me, I shift uneasily in my place. We have never before seen her come out from our side of the exit in the hall. A salutation would be a normal, instinctive response, but of course, we cannot speak and it leaves me feeling very uneasy. I look down at my feet as she passes in front of me. She is looking at the meditators bunched together near the walkway. They have been talking. She says nothing and heads into her quarters without looking back.

We head back into the stuffy hall for the last hour of afternoon meditation. I throw myself into concentrating almost immediately, lifting my thighs occasionally. My concentration is so intense that I feel like the Buddha, carved in stone. I am so deep in self-observation and the stillness is so complete, that even if a huge grasshopper were to come and sit on my arm, I would not be able to move. Stillness gives one a lot of power, I muse. Nothing can affect one if one does not react. Important lesson, I tell myself. Things affect us because we react to them. A grasshopper cannot frighten me if it comes and sits on my arm and I do not move. It will soon think of me as another immobile perch and move on. Maybe this is true for events in our lives, too. This has been Guruji's teaching and I am beginning to understand even though the waxing and waning of pain is taking a terrible toll.

As I continue meditating, happy thoughts start forming in my mind. Maybe there is a lilt in my heart because of the rain and the girl dancing with abandon, the first display of normal and carefree behaviour here in days; or maybe it is because of the secret shared by the female teacher; whatever the reason, I find myself smiling. As I do, the pain in my body wanes slightly. It is another revelation. Does happiness equal absence of pain? This sounds logical, considering the biological effect of endorphins, but I am seeing it more from the perspective of equanimity.

Maddeningly, however, I still cannot see the purpose of sitting down hour after hour just to observe changes in the body. I still wait for the mental defilements to come out. I want to feel cured, healed and wholesome. The only impactful thought I have had relate to the voices I have heard inside my head twice. But that was just succour. I have experienced fairly amazing things in my body, but these can be attributed to sharpening of the mind and senses. Is this what I have spent eight days here in silence, austerity and hardship for?

As I walk back after tea, there is a commotion in front of the female teacher's house. A snake has been found on the path right in front of her quarters. I stop to watch. Snakes do not frighten me, although I would not want one at close range. Ashram workers have been summoned, but there are no shouts or panic. One of them uses a stick to lift up the creature and flings it into the grass on the side. I am surprised but glad that the snake has not been killed. It is strange that it has been flung so close to the teacher's quarters, but it will probably slither away in the grass to a quieter place, or be grabbed before that by a peacock.

At the bend of the walkway, I am joined by the sevika, who, very astonishingly, starts chatting with me as if we are old friends and no rule of silence dominates the place. She is breathless and excited and tells me the short-haired girl has been caught talking on her cell phone and flouting other rules as well. I know that I am expected to display some shock or interest at the news and so I join in with a few hems and haws and say, 'Really?' Her excitement is quelled somewhat by such an unenthusiastic response and she soon walks away.

I am no longer angry at the sevika. There is a feeling of indulgence towards her, like that towards an errant but delightful child. My patience and tolerance towards others seems to be increasing as we near the end of the course. Maybe the feeling of resignation has lessened the frustration and agitation.

Tomorrow is the ninth day, the only 'serious' day left to work, according to Guruji. The tenth day does not really count. I know there is nothing much that I will achieve in just one more day. For all purposes, the course has ended for me. I can do some amazing stuff with my body which I can show off to others, but my spirit and mind have not been altered.

The peacock is on the same spot on the tree at the back. It looks as if it is the lord of its territory, calling out to its subjects and checking if everything is as it should be. I will miss the peacocks. I will miss this place. The serenity, the peace and the stoicism I have imbibed. I wash my face slowly and moisturize it. There is absolutely nothing else to do and it makes me reflect once again that so much of what we do in the normal course of a day is unnecessary. There is very little required for a simple, clean and healthy life: few possessions, few wants and few attachments. After that, there is no end to the cravings that can follow. I will miss this austere lifestyle. The longing and ache for my daughter is gone; I will be seeing her very soon. I just hope I can remember the ache and cherish all the moments that I will have with her from here on.

I walk slowly down the pathway, waiting for the bell to ring. I cross the triangular walkway and carry on walking, as there is a group of about seven or eight women standing there and talking loudly. I do not want to be seen around them, or let my soliloquy be interrupted. As I near the female teacher's cottage, she comes out and walking past me, goes briskly up the path towards them. I hear her scolding loudly. The women scatter like a bunch of frightened hens.

I long to keep wandering aimlessly. I have no more expectations from the technique. Nevertheless, I do not want to miss out on the now very bleak and remote possibility of further learning and an uprooting of any defilement. Hunched over, I take my seat. My back is no longer the proud and erect back it used to be. Eight days have humbled me greatly and taught me both resilience and humility.

Guruji now starts each session with the powerful words '*Anattā tan me, anattā gan me*', which mean absence of self in body and mind. Guruji sings these words with fervour and strength and they instill a brief determination and strength in me. I will remember them for months afterwards as I meditate.

Once again, I experience the waterfall effect and the quick as lightning energy flow courses down my legs; in the rest of the body, it trickles down slowly like viscous oil. I keep moving and lifting my thighs. The tiredness makes the pain worse. I have to sometimes keep them lifted up for longer durations. It must be a strange sight to anyone watching. The pain in my hips is very similar now to that of the contractions of childbirth and I wonder how I can bear them day after day and hour after hour.

The day darkens and becomes more somnolent. Crickets start their din. I wonder if I will be able to adjust to the world I left behind. At seven, we start heading out towards the mini hall. P goes up to the female teacher instead of heading out. They have a brief exchange. The teacher puts out a hand and touches P's forehead. I realize P is unwell. It is unexpected in this place; with the absence of chronic ailments. Maybe P's fever alludes – I think almost cruelly – to a weak spirit.

The American and P appear on the path together as I wait outside the Dhamma hall. The American is looking very solicitously at P. They seem to have forged a bond. The accent must be the common denominator, I muse sullenly. I turn around to watch the Aravalis slowly fading away in the light of dusk.

I sit down on my cushion gladly, leaning my back against the wall. My legs are stretched out, but away from the television set. The lone old man who used to come for the English discourse no longer comes here. I wonder why.

Guruji appears in the same old garb. He starts by saying that there is only one day left to work seriously. Even one day is enough if we work seriously, he says and advises us to keep trying to understand the technique so that we can use it properly when we go back to our homes. I am saddened at the prospect of the course coming to an end, even though it has not given me the desired outcomes. The thought of going back home is also somehow daunting.

Guruji says we must understand two important aspects of the technique; awareness and equanimity. The purpose of meditation is defeated if one is present without the other. Being aware of the gross reality relating to the physical and mental structure was not the teaching of the Enlightened One, who wanted one to work with sensations and not react to objects relating to sense tools, such as colours, sizes, shapes, sounds, smells, taste, touch and thought.

Not generating craving or aversion was not propounded by the Buddha alone. Many before him had given importance to the sense tools, but the Buddha gave importance to the sensations arising thereof. Guruji says we started with the small triangular area of the nose to make our minds sharper to be able to pick out sensations everywhere on the body so that no 'blind' areas would remain. Being able to feel sensations all over, he says, is the first important station. The second most important station is the dissolution of the entire structure of mind and matter. This is called *bhang*. Bhang happens when one's mind becomes so sharp and sensitive that the sensations first become subtler and then start getting dissolved. One starts getting a free flow of sensations within the body. I mull at this. It is true that I have a free flow of sensations within my legs all the time, but I somehow cannot correlate this to what Guruji is saying.

Guruji says the second station is very important but also dangerous. Having experienced all the gross, solidified sensations, one suddenly experiences very pleasant sensations all through the body. According to the old habit pattern of the mind, one starts developing craving. One can maintain equanimity in the face of unpleasant sensations, hoping to reach the subtler ones, but when the subtler ones come, an attachment happens towards them; it hinders the progress of vipassanā.

Some meditators, he says, keep on attending courses without understanding this and keep relishing pleasant sensations and being averse to unpleasant ones. I do not understand how anyone could choose to come back here to experience the same monotony, frightening loneliness, austerity and terrible pain. Guruji reiterates that we must get to the root level of sensations and develop equanimity towards them. This can be done only if one understands that every sensation is impermanent. With equanimity, they start changing with great rapidity and velocity. Gross, solidified sensations turn into vibrations. Though this has already happened with me, I cannot understand and accept this change.

The deepest level of the mind, Guruji says, is constantly in touch with sensations, even when one is asleep. When a mosquito bites at night, one feels an unpleasant sensation. The conscious mind would not be aware of it, but one would shift, scratch or rub. The fact that the conscious mind is not aware shows that there is a barrier between the conscious and the unconscious mind. The conscious mind keeps itself busy with objects outside at a very gross level, while the unconscious is constantly in touch with body sensations and keeps reacting to them. Unless one changes the habit pattern of the mind at the deepest level, one cannot break this barrier.

Guruji gives the example of a banyan tree seed to explain the multiplication of saṅkhāras and misery. The seed of the banyan is tiny; yet it contains a huge tree within. The banyan tree lives for centuries. Every year, it bears fruit and seeds, so that over centuries, there are thousands of seeds. Every seed, he says, has the same characteristic. Every seed has a banyan tree within. It is an endless process of multiplication. But every seed requires fertile soil and water to germinate. It cannot grow on rocky land.

A seed of a saṅkhāra also generates millions of saṅkhāras in the same way. We keep multiplying misery. It is like a spark coming into contact with a tank of gasoline. It generates millions of sparks. At the intellectual level, one can understand that one should not multiply misery. We understand that if fire is being brought towards us, we should try and extinguish the fire. However, in actuality, Guruji says, 'If someone brings fire towards us, we open our petrol tanks for the person and say burn, burn!' There is loud laughter at this and I smile, because this is so true of everyone's lives. Guruji says we throw a bucket full of petrol over the person who brings the fire. 'You burn, I burn, both of us burn,' becomes our motto, he says.

Yes, I agree silently, we burn because of others; and we burn them with us.

Each time we generate a sakhāra, Guruji says, the consciousness of the next moment arises. Material food is required for the flow of matter and mental food is required for the flow of mind. He explains this with the analogy of fasting. One can fast easily for a day. One can fast almost as easily for two days. One can even fast for a week and remain fairly healthy. One can even fast for a month, but then the body will start dying. This grave analogy reminds me of the Jain tradition of fasting unto death. It is called *Santhara* or *Sallekhana*, but it is different from suicide in the sense that it is not done under duress, but with full knowledge and intent. It is a prolonged process, which gives the person undertaking the fast time to reflect upon his or her life.

The idea may be morbid to most, but it has its appeal for me. It is a conscious way to give up one's soul and is believed to remove all negative karma and result in the highest purification of the body and mind. Jainism and Buddhism are similar in the sense that they both believe in the concept of karma; both positive and negative and in the 'inherently flawed and painful nature of existence upon the earth'.

Every moment, Guruji says, we give food to our minds. If in a moment, one does not generate a saṅkhāra, the mind flow does not stop. If, in the next moment, there is again no saṅkhāra, the mind flow still continues because of old saṅkhāras. Eventually, however, a stage comes when new saṅkhāras cease and old ones start coming out. When no new saṅkhāras are generated, one gets liberated from all misery. I am tired of hearing about saṅkhāras and misery and liberation and yet long for a stage where only old saṅkhāras will exist to subsequently be destroyed.

Guruji says when we generate anger, there is an unpleasant sensation in our body. We unconsciously react to this unpleasant sensation and thus generate a new saṅkhāra. Adding firewood to a fire keeps it burning, with the lower layers of firewood beneath. But when no more fuel is added to it, the fire consumes the remaining fuel and then dies out.

Vipassanā, Guruji says, helps us to overcome addictions. One may, for instance, be an addict of anger or an addict of misery. The equanimity inside manifests itself outside and one is able to face the vicissitudes of life with calm. If one can keep from crying in the face of grief, if one can stand steadfast when things around collapse, if one can remain stoic in the face of all odds, it is the highest beatitude. He recites a doha loudly in the style of a film song with a big smile. Translating it, he says it is easy enough to be pleasant when life flows along like a sweet song. There is loud and raucous laughter from his disciples. I reflect on how true this is. Why can we only be happy when things are going our way? Still smiling, Guruji moves his head up and down and says, 'The man worthwhile is a man with a smile, when everything goes dead wrong.' I smile broadly too and it seems like a load has been lifted from my heart. Things do go wrong for everyone. There is a smattering of applause. We are all sheepish in the face of revelation that our sorrows and pain are not as enormous as we believe or make them out to be and we express our delight and wonder like little kids whose delinquent behavior has been mocked and corrected.

When things go wrong in life, Guruji says, we have to smile. Not like actors or actresses, but from within. Even an enlightened person, he says, has to go through vicissitudes. There were many people who were against the Buddha's teachings. For the priests, it was a matter of their livelihood being threatened by the Buddha's teachings.

In the Buddha's time, it was commonplace for large opposing sects to come together to debate their beliefs. One such gathering arrived at the gates of the Buddha's ashram to discredit him. One man proffered a suggestion that the Buddha could be discredited as a religious teacher because he did not look the part. Another proffered an idea that he could be questioned on not sporting a rosary or wearing animal skins and smearing ashes on his body. But someone pointed out that these had been unsuccessful in discrediting him previously, so it was decided that they would attack his teachings.

When they examined his teachings, however, no fault could be found with the concept of sīla, for morality was the basis of all religions and not only did the Buddha preach it, he also practised it. They next examined samadhi or mastery of the mind; again, no one could find fault with trying to master one's own mind. The third foundation of the Buddha's teaching, paññā (the process by which impurities of the mind were removed) was equally irreproachable and one person in the group asked incredulously if it was actually possible to remove the impurities in one's mind, for he had never been able to do so.

They soon came to the conclusion that they could not win against the Buddha's teachings. He also did not deride other religions or philosophies and never discouraged people from their own faiths. They decided the only way to go up against the Buddha was through slander. There are only two kinds of scandals that a monk can be involved in, Guruji says, one involves money and the other involves women.

The Buddha could not be involved in a money scandal; after all, he was a prince before he renounced the world of palaces and wealth and luxury. They decided to slander him using a woman. A young and beautiful woman was sent to the ashram to pretend to be the Buddha's lover. She would tell others about the wonderful nights they spent together. After eight months, she appeared in a gathering in front of Buddha, looking heavily pregnant and shouted, 'O, shaven head! Do you have nothing for your coming child?' The powerful King Prasenjit, who was a follower of the Buddha, was in the gathering; so were a lot of other prominent and important people.

The Buddha could have told King Prasenjit that the woman was a liar and to have her severely punished. But he only smiled and said, 'O, my child, you and I both know the truth.' Upon hearing this, the woman became so nervous that the piece of wood she had tied around her stomach fell off and her lie was exposed. At this, Guruji says delightedly, 'See, Dhamma works!' and this, for once, is truly funny. I laugh and shake my head.

Once, Guruji says, an old Brahmin came to the Buddha's abode in a rage because he believed that the Buddha's teachings had corrupted his family's beliefs and rituals. He advanced towards the Buddha with a sword in his hand, spouting profanity. The Buddha remained unperturbed and asked him to sit down and discuss the matter. Knowing the Buddha was trying to calm him down, the Brahmin refused to discuss anything. The Buddha then asked the old man if any visitors came to his house. Though the furious Brahmin did not want to reply, he answered that they did and it was none of the Buddha's business. The Buddha, however, continued and asked him if the visitors brought presents. Again, in spite of himself and still advancing towards the Buddha, the Brahmin answered that they did and demanded to know what business it was of the Buddha.

Unrelenting, the Buddha asked what happened to the presents if the Brahmin did not like them. The Brahmin answered that he would send them back with the one who came bearing them. Upon hearing this, the Buddha said that he also did not want to accept the presents that the Brahmin had got for him. As he relates this, Guruji waves his hand as if shooing an animal away and once again there is light laughter. Realization dawns on the old Brahmin. Throughout our lives, whenever people bring us unwanted presents of hate and animosity, we only seek to give them back manifold to them, instead of refusing to react. He lowered his sword and became a disciple of the Buddha.

I glance at the clock. It is almost time for the discourse to end. Guruji says there are four kinds of people in the world: those who move from darkness to darkness, those who regress from brightness to darkness, those who advance from darkness to brightness, and those who move from brightness to brightness.

People who move from darkness to darkness are people who are cursed with ill luck, but they also spend their lives with hate, anger and resentment towards their fate. They pave the way for further darkness. People who regress from brightness to darkness are those who have been blessed with everything life can offer: family, money, status and health, but they ruin it all. People who advance from darkness to brightness have misery and suffering in their lives, but their wisdom guides them to live their lives with compassion and love. Their present was darkness, but their future would be bright.

Lastly, Guruji says, there are those people who move from brightness to brightness. Blessed with all that is good, they still keep planting the seeds of brightness in their minds and lives. They understand that their good fortune is the result of good karma and that they must make use of it for the good of others.

Like the Buddha, Guruji is also a person who has chosen to go from brightness to brightness. Both were born in wealthy families and both chose to forsake wealth and comforts for a life devoted to helping others.

Which category do I fit in, I wonder? I am scared I may have fallen in the brightness to darkness category or I may also be heading from darkness to darkness. The thought frightens me and I vow to myself that I will head towards brightness irrespective of from where I have sprung.

I do not still really believe in the concept of karma, but even I have no way of explaining why ill luck befalls a good person and a bad person is blessed with good fortune. There has to be some explanation. Nevertheless, the description of four kinds of people makes me understand that no one is responsible for my sorrow but me. It is I who has to decide my life and fate and plant seeds of brightness.

With this, the discourse is over. The path outside is wet. P is looking very unwell. She is walking with the American. Surprisingly, the American is talking to her in a low voice. I am astounded. I have seen many women break the rule of silence, especially in the last two days, but I expected better from her. Is the nearing of the end of the course making everybody stray from the path of righteousness? Whatever the reason, I feel left out. If the American and P can talk, why not me? I am also genuinely concerned about P now. I catch up with them on the path and ask P in a low voice if she has a fever. She replies she has been unwell for a couple of days. I then ask if she has taken any medicine for it. Instead of answering clearly, she mumbles something and then says,

'We will talk day-after, when we are allowed to.' P's abrupt response stuns me into silence and I let her walk on with the American. I feel foolish for having spoken to her. It adds to my dejection.

My wisdom is being undermined by unreason. My disillusionment at the absence of any tangible, wholesome gains has grown. I decide to speak to the male teacher again. Once I am seated at his feet in the hall, I start by telling him I have experienced many things Guruji has spoken about: dissolution of pain, the 'cascade effect' and the lightning-like energy streams down my legs. He nods his head approvingly and says, 'That's very good,' and then suddenly corrects himself, realizing, like I do, that one is supposed to be neutral towards sensations. I smile inwardly. Teachers are fallible, after all and I suppose I am still sulking about his condemnation of my experience with levitation and my equating the technique with self-flagellation.

When I ask him once again what the purpose of all these experiences is, he says the cascade effect is temporary and I may again feel intense pain in my legs. He tells there will be subsequent courses for me to expand my learning. I balk at the assumption. Shaking my head firmly, I tell him I will never be coming back. He does not respond. I thank him and walk away.

I have come to the end of something I had great belief and hope in. I wanted to become a different person: strong and invincible. I wanted defilements to be wrenched out of my mind. But all I have now is a sense of resignation. Yes, my sorrows do not seem as huge as they did before coming here because everything seems to be maya or illusion. I will be gone one day like all of us and all the pain, regret, shame, bitterness, anger and hate will be nothing; even though Dhamma would like me to believe that negative volitions live on in the afterlife.

I meditate while thinking despondent thoughts. My

hip joints and right knee are revolting. Lifting my thighs gives no relief to my knee. I look forward to retiring to the room, even though the ending of the day means only one day will now be left to attain any kind of spiritual revelation or breakthrough.

I walk back without looking at the sky. I will soon be back in the world of aeroplanes and people. Beyond the residential block, there is some construction going on and the sound is loud and jarring in the night. The pace of activity seems to be frenzied. The construction coming up near the ashram will destroy a lot of the peace and quiet and I feel sorry for those who will be meditating here in the years to come. One day, the Aravalis will also be hidden from view, or broken down for mining and quarrying. Everything is Anicca.

I muse quietly while I go about my nightly chores in the room. I have not been a quitter. I have borne suffering for eight days and I have two more to go. I have remained resilient. I have followed the precepts of sīla well, and now I think that the killing of the ticks and the stealing of the pen and paper was probably not a very big violation. After all, people have broken the vow of silence, been absent from adhishtan, combined vipassanā with religious rituals and not meditated sincerely when they should have. My sīla has been good, even if my meditation has not been perfect.

It is difficult for me to accept anything less than perfect or ideal in myself, but I now have to confront the truth. I put up the mosquito net with a feeling of acute loneliness and dismal bleakness and slip inside. I think of Guruji's words about saṅkhāras. Subconsciously, I start observing sensations again. Energy streams strongly down my legs, abdomen and arms. Guruji has spoken about a stage when vibrations would be felt beneath gross sensations. Wondering if I could have reached that stage, I start concentrating on my knee. I can feel some sensations on it, which are independent of the excruciating pain. I concentrate wholly upon it like never before.

Suddenly, it feels I have penetrated the barrier of the skin and slipped inside, into muscle and sinew, like a knife through flesh. My mind can automatically follow the currents of pain inside, from right to left. The knife probes further, relentlessly. I am now not aware of anything but the layers of flesh and the pain between those layers. I have almost stopped breathing because of the effort and am barely aware I am alive. The knife keeps cutting away at the layers and suddenly, there is no more pain. I pull my mind out from the depths of the flesh and start panting. It is like I have cauterized the pain with the knife of my mind. This experience is even more wondrous than that of the 'white light'. Not only have I gone beneath the skin, I have also managed to draw out the pain like a surgeon.

I now divert my whole being to the few square inches of my back where the pain is the most intense. Unlike with the knee, the piercing does not happen laterally, but straight down, as if a needle has been thrust in. It goes in deeper and deeper and then suddenly bounces off a hard surface and diverts sharply to the left. With a start, I realize I have hit the shoulder blade. Beads of sweat break out on my skin as the enormity of what has happened sinks in. I have penetrated inside my body till the bone.

I am like a mad scalpel-wielding surgeon now, testing the limits of my capability. I start from the top of my body and proceed downwards, concentrating intently on small areas at a time. I am now beneath the surface of the skin all over my body. The energy stream deflects off my ribs and my knife slips into the cavity of my chest to pick out the flapping movement of the diaphragm.

I am no longer agitated and desperate. Calm is settling in. I have been unable to do adhishtan for an hour. I have been unable to rid myself of mental defilements. I will have to face the same truths when I go back to my world and I do not know if I will be able to deal with them any better than I have so far. I can accept everything now. I start speaking audibly, breaking the precept of noble silence. My voice is low enough not to carry out of the room and the whirring of the noisy fans also ensures I will not be heard.

Okay, I tell myself. I have not achieved what I came here for. But these days here have given me strength and a belief in my resilience. That is not bad. I have had a refuge and shelter for my wounded soul; albeit short-lived. In this refuge, I have taken pleasures in simple things like blue flowers and peacock feathers. I have developed a deeper respect for my fellow humans, even when I have felt scorn for their weaknesses and envy for their strengths.

I have found friends for life: the American, the Italian, the girl in flared pants and P. We have developed an unspoken but powerful bond as soul sisters; having been through the same trials. I have had a natural and healthy diet all these days and it must have helped detoxify my body. I have experienced miracles with my body and I now know it as a truly alive entity, even if it is really only a farcical physical structure. This experience has still been an experience of a lifetime and a book still may come out of it, if those wet and loose pages come together some day.

I am behaving like a vipassanā meditator. When confronted with unexpected and unpleasant circumstances, one sets about trying to salvage the best out of them. Tomorrow, I shall wake up without regret. It is all finished for me, but it has been fulfilling. I shall miss this place when I leave and forever be grateful for the time I have spent here.

I am now ready for sleep. I get out of bed for a sip of water and glance at the courtyard. The sevika is unlocking the gate. I watch as she opens it and steps out to join a young man who is waiting outside. My mouth falls open. Is this a rendezvous? It is half past eleven, very late even for the sevika. She closes the gate and is gone.

I do not care what the sevika is up to. What people do here or anywhere else is their business. The young man might be her brother or somebody from the ashram who has work with her. I am at peace for the first time in days and tomorrow will be the last day of meditation. The thought makes me sorrowful for a few seconds till I realize everything is impermanent: this course, pain and even life.

10

ADHISHTAN

❦

Day Nine

*T*ODAY IS THE LAST DAY IN WHICH I CAN EXPECT ANYTHING to happen, but I am not too hopeful. Still, I am at peace. When there is no more expectation, there is acceptance and thus there is peace.

The early morning before dawn is very quiet and peaceful as I walk towards the hall and I can hear the evocative and haunting call of *azaan*, the Muslim call for prayer. I will miss this early morning communion with nature, with the higher being, with the self. I am acutely aware of just how much loneliness and solitude I have gone through in the past eight days. Tomorrow the vow of silence will be lifted, but I do not have any words left and no need either to communicate with anyone. My friend told me laughingly I would be calling him on the tenth day. I hope he understands if I don't, simply because I have no desire to communicate.

Having accepted the inevitable last night, I decide to now meditate seriously. I have nothing to lose. Most of my upper body pain is gone, but the right knee and hip joints are still in agony. Even though I have experienced the regular waxing and waning of pain in keeping with the laws of anicca, my body is afire with pain every time I sit down.

Lifting of the thighs helps me carry on sitting for about forty minutes, but eventually, the pain gets too intense and I have to open out my legs. The meditation goes well, however. I get little 'waterfall effects' and I shiver with the intense vibrations. My mind traverses from the top of my thigh to the toes in a flash. And now I go deeper into the skin and within my body. At places, the energy on the surface just slices through the flesh and I can feel the surfaces of organs inside. On my neck, I no longer just feel a pricking on the surface. The sensations carry on into my throat and touch my oesophagus. They don't stop there, but break into the hollow of the pipe. It is a wondrous feeling, but I am conscious of the fact that enjoying sensations is dangerous and counter-productive. I feel an urge to linger inside the oesophagus, but force myself to move on.

I hear the curtains being opened and realize it is dawn. I have wetness beneath my closed eye lids and a lump in my throat. I have felt a great sense of protection and succour here even without a single companion and I can only hope I can withstand the storms that I expect back in the world beyond the boundary of the ashram. At six, the singing starts. The words are different today. The word Dhamma is repeated loudly many times and it jars in my head each time. Finally, at half past six we move out towards the dining hall. I have almost no appetite and now I carefully observe every action and the impact of each stimulus upon the sense organs. As I eat, I feel the morsels upon my tongue in a way I have never felt them before and can observe the sensations in the mouth. Whether I lift up my spoon or stretch out my legs, I can feel every action as if it is broken down into its component parts.

The old, hunched lady appears in front of me and my eye goes to her wrist, where her plain glass bangles are now tied together with a bit of rope. I feel a deep sadness as I look at the rope. It is because of me that they have been tied.

Sometimes, those who we think have caused us injustice or harm may not even be aware that they have done so. And we spend our lives in needless animosity, bitterness, resentment and hate.

I look briefly in the direction of the Aravalis. Two days from now, I will be free to roam those hills. Only, we are never really free even when we are, because of the bondages we choose for ourselves. I will go back to my old life, to live the same hopes, fears and dreams.

I feel like washing my hair but realize it is better to leave it for tomorrow. Tomorrow, I shall wear my hair loose with the pretty polka dotted headband that I have carried with me. Tomorrow, we will relate to each other as normal people again. I shall wear kohl in my eyes. It will be a sort of celebration for the course ending. I am excited at the thought of dressing up.

I bathe and change. I carefully fold my dirty laundry and place it at the bottom of the bag: I am going home! When I emerge for my customary stroll at a quarter past seven, a peacock crosses the path in front of me and hops over to the other side. I smile a wistful smile. My journey of meditation and peacock feathers is done.

In the meditation hall, all traces of excitement and composure vanish. Guruji tells us to try and pierce and penetrate the whole body after we get pleasant and uniform sensations all over. All I have is the erratic free flow and the fiery pain in my hips and legs. Does this mean others have progressed way beyond me? The confusion and agitation throws my meditation totally out of gear. I notice the pain gets more severe when I am agitated and I struggle for equilibrium in my mind. I try to penetrate my body, but I can only think of the pain, and my endeavour is entirely unsuccessful. I do not bother to exercise in the break. Pain is all in the mind.

In the next sitting, Guruji says something about dissolving

the entire physical structure of the body. This throws me into further disarray. A state of dissolution is unfathomable when my body is screaming for succour. The instructions go on till ten o'clock. I change my pose many times and my body is exhausted and quivering when I head out gratefully in the break. Unfortunately, the break is too short and we are soon summoned back into the hall.

It feels like I am sitting atop a raging fire. If I remain still, I 'burn' slowly but if I move often to relieve the pain or get distracted otherwise, the flames rage and spit. But even a drop of sweat on the body is a humongous distraction which upsets the fine balance of the body and it is difficult to not move at all. I give up and slump over before eleven. Knowing it is impossible to continue, I walk out and head very slowly towards the dining hall. I am the first one to reach and am told to wait outside till the gong rings. I sit near the water cooler, mulling over going back to the teacher in the afternoon to clear the confusion over the latest instructions.

After lunch, I head straight for the hall. There are not too many people in the meditation hall at question hour today. It seems most of them have just given up. The male teacher is occupied with a student and the female teacher is unoccupied, but I wait before the male teacher. The female teacher does not seem in the least offended and in fact, gesticulates to ask if I want my questions to be answered by him. I nod my head, grateful that I have not hurt her feelings.

When the male teacher allows me audience, I ask him about the new instructions regarding dissolution of the body. He smiles and says I should not worry; those are mostly for future courses and I should just observe sensation in the body. I reiterate firmly once again that I will not be coming back. He looks unblinkingly at me for a few seconds. Then, he reassures me that I am not falling behind in the course. For once, the reassurance works.

As I cross the female teacher, she asks me how things are going and I reply all is well, because even if I wanted to, I could not have described my feelings at this point in time. I also reply that I was confused about an aspect of the technique; thus the audience with the male teacher. At this, she smiles and says it is all really quite simple. All that is required is to observe, recognize and remain calm. The way she says it really does make the whole process sound exceedingly simple. It is, in fact, the whole body of the technique. Observe sensations as they are; recognize their impermanence and maintain equanimity. Why can't I do just that? I nod my head at her and leave the hall.

In my room, I think about her words. Maybe I have been complicating things too much. The only problem is the blasted pain, which sends all rationality and logic and common sense out of the window. Still, I am calmer now and aim to execute this simple philosophy in the next session of meditation.

I manage to grab a few winks. On the way to the hall for the next four hour session, I feel I am tottering, but the teacher's words give me hope. I resolve I shall meditate till two and then loiter outside till adhishtan at half past two.

I hold on for quite a while in the cross-legged position; calming my mind with the words the female teacher has spoken. It works for a while, till the hip pain goes out of control. I have seen that this happens mostly when I get anxious about the time. The biggest nīvaraña now is anxiety about time. When I perceive that the time for the sitting to get over is drawing close, my equilibrium goes completely awry and the suppressed and controlled pain breaks out in showers of agony.

I put my head down between my knees. It is not even two o'clock. Others still have their eyes closed and I marvel at them and envy them their resilience. However, I know now this is my own personal battle. Comparison is useless and futile because everyone experiences things differently.

I move out of the hall and look around for peacocks. There are none about, so I stand in the shade of the tin roof which houses the cooler. Adhishtan sessions are easier in one aspect: the presence of the teachers. Even though they mostly meditate as rigorously as us, one always gets the feeling one is being watched. Also, the period ends definitively. There is no ambiguity about time. It makes for better motivation.

Meditators now start coming out singly and in groups. I notice some walk less painfully than others and there are some who look as if they have been through a mangle. In breaks, when I am up and about, I am no longer in pain. This is because the back pain I have endured for so many days is gone and my legs only start cramping and numbing when I sit. The only part which aches dully all the time is the pelvic girdle. This dull ache flares up to alarming and unbearable proportions when I start meditating. However, this too, subsides and peaks now. I remember Guruji saying this would happen 'with greater velocity', in one of the discourses.

Minutes after I sit down for adhishtan, my legs numb. I have to ignore the numbness now, because I have discovered a painful fact. When I lift up my thighs to relieve the pain; unlike before, an excruciating shower of pins and needles follows. If the pins and needles do not happen when I move, the numbness becomes twice as bad. It is as alarming as the cobra in my back, which, when I used to move or twist my back to escape it; would uncoil itself further and raise its hood.

I thus valiantly ignore the numbness. Slowly, it grows in intensity, even though I explore my body keeping as still and calm as I can. The tightness in my legs has become worse than the hip pain. I dread succumbing to temptation and lifting up my thighs, for that will bring more pain. I remind myself of the teacher's words: observe and recognize impermanence.

Maintain equanimity in the knowledge that pain is fleeting. I carry on, pushing myself to the brink in much the same way as I did when I experienced the 'white light'. I wonder if the pain is going to disappear miraculously. It does not. I am now crying inside with the effort of holding on, but now my legs are so heavy that I cannot move them even if I want to. Now all I can do is believe in anicca with all my being.

I force myself to move back to the top of my head and follow the snaking vibrations downwards. As I do this with beads of sweat inflaming my whole body with sensation, I suddenly feel a slow, spontaneous release of pins and needles in my legs: not the agonizing burst that causes tremendous pain, but a controlled unloading of the dead weight. These are bubbly, pleasant tickles and I can barely breathe at the wonder of this phenomenon. I am so stupefied and so afraid that observing them will unbalance my mind and make my legs dead weight again that I force my attention back to my upper body. I register vaguely that my legs are 'cooling down' more and more.

It is as always more difficult to describe the slow release of pain, especially in this slow, symmetrical, even fashion, than it is to describe something as rapid as the 'white light'. While the 'white light' was like a hurricane; rushing in with all its power, the slow release of pain is like a tumultuous tide receding slowly from the beach and going back into the sea. They are both miraculous and amazing experiences in their own way, but what makes this one very special is that in the process of holding on and the spontaneous cooling of the body while I continue concentrating, the voice of Guruji comes on and announces 'anicca, anicca'. The hour is up. And for the first time in the course, on the day before it ends, I have completed adhishtan. I have remained unmoving for an hour.

No words can quite express the conquering of a summit after all hope of reaching the peak is long gone. I had no expectation left from the last two days of the course and there had been a quiet, resigned acceptance of my fallibility. Yet, I did not slacken. Had this been a reward for my quiet, accepting surrender? Maybe it was all about equanimity: in those moments when I forced my attention back to other parts of the body, my mind attained its balance and maybe all those moments added up towards the coveted goal: adhishtan.

I long to share with the world that I have succeeded, but this longing is different from the urge of wanting to share the experience of the 'white light'. This is quieter and far more beauteous. And even as the sunshine of freedom from the bondage of many wasted years shines within me, I maintain the same stoic and expressionless face that I have for the last nine days.

I have completed adhishtan according to the dictates of vipassanā. The girl who could not sit cross-legged for more than ten minutes nine days ago has managed a complete hour of sitting, with the worst kind of pain imaginable. It gives resilience and courage a new name and I am proud I have been blessed with that courage. I am now a different being. I am not the aspirant and the spiritual struggler who entered the ashram ten days ago. I am tathāgata. I am free. It has all come together in a beauteous, awesome manner.

It feels like I have broken free and the useless shell of my confined existence lies broken under the hot August sun. I watch butterflies upon the hedge leading to the pagoda and I feel more alive than I have in many years. I want to genuflect and place my forehead upon the dry earth of this place that has soaked up my pain, but I only stand and gaze unseeingly into the distance. I cannot cry and I cannot rejoice. The sense of fulfilment has suffused my being to an extent that I am devoid of all emotion.

As I sit lost in the wonder of it all in the hall, Guruji's voice comes on. It is unusual for this time of day. The period is not one of adhishtan. Guruji has some more instructions. After reaching a state of dissolution or bhang, he says, one should try and penetrate and dissolve the last bastion: the spinal cord. Then the body would be nothing but a mass of moving particles. This, however, would not be the ultimate state as gross and solidified sensations could appear even after this. These would be old, deep-rooted saṅkhāras from past lives and would only be eradicated if one remained unreacting even at this stage.

I try not to think about these stages that are impossible for me to attain during this course. I have already achieved what I came here for. It does not matter where I go from here. I have tested the limits of my strength and emerged victorious. Nothing will ever be as difficult as this again.

It is around four in the evening by the time Guruji's instructions finish. There is an hour more to go and I try once again for adhishtan but am unsuccessful. I am not overly disappointed, knowing now that everything is fleeting and passing. When I emerge at tea time, I am at peace. It is a kind of peace I have not known for years.

Evening adhishtan after tea is the most poignant today. I know my time here is rapidly drawing to an end. We will be allowed to leave at half past six in the morning on the eleventh day. And tomorrow we will be allowed to speak and to communicate with the world outside. I am apprehensive about this transition back into a world that I left a few days back. It seems like another life now.

The peacocks call loudly and peahens answer intermittently, as if they are shy to express their amour. I cannot manage adhishtan, but I have *real* peace inside; the kind of peace Guruji wished us to have.

It is time for the discourse. Tomorrow morning, we will not have to communicate through telepathy, but I do not know if that will be better than the unspoken communication which has served us well all these days.

As I walk to the mini hall, I think about my book. Maybe I can still write it. After all, I have the perfect ending for the story.

I sit down in my usual place in the hall and the television set is switched on. I sit contentedly with a glow inside me, which I am sure is reflected on my face. Guruji appears on the screen. I have come to revere this man who tells childish stories and gives funny examples and mispronounces words and groans at the end of sentences and dohas. He has acquired the status of a demigod in my eyes, though I am aware he would cringe at the allusion to divinity. He calls himself only an acharya or teacher.

Guruji begins by saying we need to understand now how to use vipassanā in our daily lives; otherwise it would become relegated to being just another forgotten ritual. He recommends that we continue practising it for an hour in the morning and an hour in the evening. The thought of having to continue the painful meditation even at home fills me with dread, but if this is what Guruji recommends, this is what I will do. Guruji says that sitting mechanically, experiencing sensations, would not help. If the practice of meditation did not change the way we reacted in our daily life, it would mean there was something wrong in the way it was being practised.

Some change, he says, has to come about. Unwanted things would happen; wanted things would not happen. People would treat us badly. We would still react to all this unpleasantness. But it would be worth noting whether there was any difference in the way we reacted. Nine times out of ten, we would probably react in a similar way as before; but not reacting in the same fashion even one single time would mean the technique was helping. The frequency of such episodes would slowly increase. Previously, if we remained hurt or angry for eight hours, we might remain hurt or angry for only six after practising vipassanā. Thus, we would have gained two hours. There is laughter. I am intrigued.

Guruji explains that the duration of negative reactions would automatically decrease over time, even if respiration or sensation was not observed while reacting. This was the law of nature. If we practised vipassanā in the proper way, we would stop experiencing elation at pleasant occurrences and dejection at unpleasant ones. I think about my endless battle with sorrow. If this happens, I tell myself, I will experience the highest beatitude that Guruji has spoken about: the eradication of my melancholy.

With the understanding of anicca, Guruji says, there is an increase in equanimity. Even if we didn't observe our respiration or sensations in a particular situation, a part of our mind would automatically observe what was happening within and help us overcome negativity faster. In an hour, if we watched even once how we were reacting by observing respiration or the sensations within, we would gain a few moments of equanimity. These moments would add up and start reversing the process of reacting negatively to adverse situations in our life.

It is like a car travelling at high speed and about to collide with something, Guruji says. If the brake is applied even once, the speed decreases and the damage is lessened. We should not expect, however, that we would soon become perfect beings. The lessening of the intensity and duration of our negative reactions would be enough. It would be progress on the path of Dhamma, even if it was slow.

It is ignorance, Guruji says, that makes us wallow in misery. No one wants to be unhappy. Enlightened people advised others to observe negativity, not suppress it or indulge it. This was the middle path, to observe, whether it was fear, anger, passion, worry or pain. Observing the *object* of the anger or sadness only compounded negativity. The only solution was to look within.

We spend all our lives thinking that the cause of our misery lies outside. A husband might feel if his wife changed herself even a little, the household would become heaven. The wife might feel the same way about her husband. People keep wishing for others to change, so that they can have a peaceful and happy environment and life, but all the energy used in trying to rectify things outside is a waste. It is very difficult to try and change others or alter circumstances to suit our needs. Even if one ruled the world, one would not be able to make all circumstances perfect. Then again, there was no guarantee that if a person changed or a circumstance improved, another unwanted situation would not arise.

The path, Guruji says, is full of thorns and pebbles. The only sensible solution, he says, is to wear shoes. There is loud laughter at this statement and I shake my head in admiration at Guruji's practical wisdom.

This is what we have started doing by practising vipassanā, Guruji says. Paññā tells us the whole truth, not just partial, distorted truth associated with our suffering. When one observes the whole truth, delusions go away. If five blind people are brought to an elephant and asked to describe it, all five will have different versions of the appearance of the creature, depending on which part they have examined. One may describe the elephant as a broom or brush because he touches the tail; another may describe the elephant as a pillar or post by feeling its leg. Though both are partly true, neither will be anywhere close to the real truth.

Guruji says we have started observing two dimensions to our misery; external and internal. As we progress, he says, we will be able to reach a stage where these would assume equal proportions. Finally, we would reach a stage of realization that the entire source of our suffering is internal. That is the stage, Guruji says, where we would assume responsibility for it and the whole pattern of our lives would change.

It is our reactions that determine our suffering, Guruji

explains. We may not like a person, but others may react to the same person differently. It is all within. When a person hurts us, he wants us to be unhappy at that time, but we remain unhappy for years, reliving that moment in our minds a hundred times. We resolve that we will never forget or forgive! The audience laughs and Guruji says this is madness. To suffer once is a big mistake. To suffer many times for no reason is madness.

We may react in different ways to the same occurrence, he says. He enunciates this with the help of a beautiful example, which will impact and influence my thinking greatly. In one situation, he says, he is walking in the dark with a group of his students and one of them trips over a person lying on the path. This person lets out expletives at the student. This situation, Guruji says, will not affect him, rather it would reinforce his belief that he, the great vipassanā teacher, was superior to his clumsy students. In a second situation, Guruji says, he is walking alone and he is the one who trips over the person lying on the path. The same expletives are hurled. The sound and purpose of the words is the same, but this time, it affects him, because the words are directed at him – a great vipassanā teacher.

In a third situation, he is again the one to trip over the person, but this time his students are present. This situation is even more unpleasant for him, as the students hear their great teacher being humiliated. In a fourth situation, he again trips over the person. He is alone, but the person hurling the expletives is his beloved son. This causes a very intense unpleasant sensation in him because his own son is abusing him. In a fifth and last situation, the person he trips over is again the son, but this time his students are also with him. This time, Guruji says, the unpleasantness knows no bounds.

Why does the same occurrence cause so many different reactions when the person being tripped over is the same and does not know the person who has tripped over him? Why does it cause different levels of unpleasantness? It is because of the image we create of ourselves in our minds and also the image we create of ourselves in others' minds. We develop a lot of attachment to this self-image. In the first situation, Guruji says, his own image is enhanced in his eyes, because the idea that he himself cannot err is reinforced. In the second situation, there is an unpleasant reaction because his self-image takes a beating.

In the third situation, the reaction is more severe, because not only does his own self-image take a beating, the image he has carved of himself in his students' minds also takes a beating. This is what we all do, Guruji says. Not only do we create a noble and perfect image of ourselves in our own minds, we also place that image in others' minds. Any injury or blemish to that image shatters our peace. In the fourth situation, the unpleasantness is huge, because his self-image gets blemished and the person blemishing it is his own son. In the fifth situation, the unpleasantness knows no bounds because not only does his self-image take a beating in the eyes of his students, the image of his son in their eyes also gets shattered. What is different about them that they should merit different reactions? But this is how we go about our lives, constantly getting affected by what reinforces or undermines our self-image and the image of what or who is dear to us.

Guruji now explains *pāramīs,* qualities or virtues that help us reach our goal of liberation. The first of these, Guruji says, is the quality of renunciation. It is not as easy for householders to renounce the material world to meditate in earnest. In the ashram, one is given an opportunity to live the life of a monk or a nun and also to live on the charity of others, in order to develop the spirit of humility.

The second pāramī, Guruji explains, is the quality of virtue or morality. During the course, one is given almost no opportunity to break one's sīla. The third is the pāramī of effort. This, of course, is developed here to an extraordinary level, when we sit and meditate for ten and a half hours every day. The fourth is the pāramī of wisdom. Staying here and practising the technique has taught us living wisdom – wisdom experienced by the self, within one's own body and mind.

The fifth is the quality of tolerance. Guruji says during these ten days, some meditators would try not to disturb others, but the others would not care. Then again, in the long hours in the meditation hall and elsewhere, there would be constant coughing and burping and movement and one would continually get disturbed, but slowly, the realization that negativity breeds agitation would set in and one would continue with one's efforts regardless. This has certainly happened with me. I remember being irritated and disturbed by the sound of women talking and sweeping during meditation hours and also by the sounds and smells in the hall and how I gradually came to accept and tolerate them and remain unmoved by them. How glorious it would be if we could do this all the time in our daily lives.

The sixth pāramī, Guruji says, is the pāramī of *sacca*, the virtue of truth – the truth experienced by oneself. The seventh is the *adhitthana* pāramī. He says all of us are only too familiar with this pāramī, which translates into 'I won't run away; I will observe all the rules; I will sit for one hour unmoving, each time and I will bear the most terrible pain quietly.' I smile. Guruji tells us that the Buddha excelled in this pāramī. He sat down with a vow that he would not get up from his meditation till he attained enlightenment, even if it meant his bones would turn to dust.

All of us here know that determination and resolve has kept us here for these ten days, which have been equivalent to a lifetime. To bear untold pain and mental agony silently, day after day, is a true feat of courage. I am proud that I have proved my mettle.

Mettā pāramī, Guruji continues, is the virtue of love for all beings. We all know of the adage 'love thy neighbour', but very few of us live by it. At the surface level, we may try and put it into practice, but deep down, the negativity and hostility stays. The unconscious mind being much stronger than the conscious, it never really goes away. Tomorrow, Guruji says, we will learn how to share loving kindness with others through mettā meditation.

The ninth virtue, Guruji says, is equanimity. Like the pāramī of determination, this is something that has been instilled into us in the last ten days. If only all of us can remember to constantly strive for it when we leave here. In our daily life, we can attain equanimity at the surface level. Here, through intense meditation, we have attained it at the deepest level of the mind.

The tenth pāramī, Guruji says, is that of *dana*, or charity. Our egos grow bigger as we accumulate more and more wealth. Sharing our good fortune with others is the noblest way to lessen our ego. Of course, the giving should be completely selfless. Guruji says that the donation we may choose to give at the end of the course to pay for others' boarding and lodging would be an example of true dana, because it would be given without any expectation. Dana could also be given in kind, for example, in the form of voluntary service such as the one done by the sevaks and sevikas.

Guruji raises his hand and says softly, 'May all your pāramīs develop. May you all reach the final goal – liberation from all bondages and defilements.' I feel like saying 'amen', but of course, the last words here are the ones for which all of us reverentially switch back to the lotus pose: 'Bhavatu sabba mangalam'; ending with the word 'sadhu'.

As I walk back to the meditation hall, I drink in the sights and sounds and smells of the ashram, trying to imprint them in my mind. I do not attempt conversation with P or anyone else. There will be enough time tomorrow.

The Hindi discourse is getting over just as we reach the hall. I gaze across at the little expanse, which will always be my sanctuary and almost envy those who will come after me. I enter the hall with a will I have not displayed for many days now. There are only twenty minutes left to meditate. I close my eyes and meditate with a mixed sense of peace and sadness. My pain is subdued now; even the hip pain has subsided, as if sensing that the worst is already over.

The male teacher announces that the vow of silence will be lifted the following morning at ten, but we should take care not to talk inside or around the meditation hall and that the female and male segregation should continue in the same manner.

I head back slowly to my room, lingering at the sight of the pagoda, which shimmers dully in the dark. I bow my head in reverence. Today is the only day apart from the second day that I have not cried and tonight I shall sleep without any emotional upheaval in my heart. There is no more questioning and no more pain.

I lie in my bed and look at the sky from the window. My eyes are now alert and wise, from which a lot of the pain has been bleached away. Unfortunately, so has a lot of elation and there never will be stars in them again. I sleep peacefully in my hot, stuffy little room – a deep, dreamless and soundless sleep.

11

Re-entering the World

❦

Day Ten

On the last day, I wake up peacefully, before the bell. The meditation hall, which I have dreaded for so many days, seems now a quiet haven where I have found my truth and liberation. I sit peacefully in the cross-legged position and lose myself in the task of meditating. There is a strong electric flow in my body, like a constant current of mild voltage and I wonder where it was, all these years. I am used to the coming and going of pain and so I ignore a slight flaming of pain in my back and knee. The hip pain is bad, but I ignore that as well. It is best left alone, when it sulkily quietens itself and leaves me to my task.

I aim for adhishtan. I know it is possible and today is the last day I can push myself to my limits. I resist the urge to calculate time or move in the slightest. When I finally open my eyes, estimating that an hour must surely be up and turn to look at the clock in the back of the hall, my eyes grow wide. It is a quarter to six! I have meditated unmoving for an hour and fifteen minutes; fifteen minutes more than the stipulated time for adhishtan! I stare uncomprehendingly at the clock for a few moments and then turn around to look at my co-meditators. Most are sprawled in various poses of distress.

I unfold my legs. The wonderment of what has happened and the evocative beauty of the dawn cannot keep me confined to the meditation hall any more. I rise softly and head out.

It is a dawn I will remember for years. I soak in the beauty like a dry sponge and feel like pirouetting in the early morning chill. I am the only one outside but I do not care that I will be missing forty more minutes of meditation. Peace and grace fill my being. Unfortunately, it is short lived, because a horde of monkeys comes scampering at full speed from the direction of the dining hall towards me. I recoil in horror and fright. All peace and grace forgotten, I scamper inside and with great relief close the door. I am angry at the monkeys for having ruined a very special moment, but then smile at the situation and sit down. It is nearly six and soon the dohas begin. I cannot meditate, so I sit with my legs to a side, eyes open, waiting impatiently for the recital to finish.

I walk faster to the dining hall than I have in days. The slow, contemplative gait of the past few days is gone, though I am still observing my actions and movements. I eat breakfast slowly. There seems to be no pressing hurry anymore. After I am done, I stand outside to read the notice board. A detailed schedule for the last day is on it. I read that there is an adhishtan session at eight, after which there will be *mangal maitreyi*, also known as mettā meditation or the meditation of loving kindness, at nine. At ten, we will be allowed to collect our phones and belongings from the office. The vow of silence will be lifted at ten and we will be free to venture outside the space which we have been confined to. I feel both fearful and excited.

There are many other notices today. There is one about guidelines regarding mingling with co-meditators and the usage of phones after the vow of silence is lifted and one regarding cleaning our rooms and taking off the covers of our respective cushions in the meditation hall and in the pagoda cells. Another specifies several other guidelines. There is also the thought for the day. After so many days of not having had anything to read except one or two notices, this feels like an information overload. The tenth day is preparing us to leave as fast as day zero prepared us for the following ten days.

I bathe quickly and happily. I am going to be dressing up. I look forward to looking a bit like my old self again, even though I have never before experienced the liberation of not having to look my best all the time. I have been so comfortable in my natural self. When we take off our masks, our true natures are revealed and we become free of the forced façades that we wear as protective armour.

I don the headband with a little smile on my face. My face seems a little pinched, but I am happy and I feel festive. I wear the kohl carefully and it is hard to describe in words how I feel when I do so. It is akin to how a bride might feel on her wedding day. I step out into the glorious sunshine and smile at the peacocks. It is almost eight o' clock. I do not look forward to meditation, but I also do not recoil at the thought of it anymore. This is going to be the last sitting.

Since, in my estimate, I have already achieved the pinnacle of success after the hour and fifteen minute long adhishtan today, I no longer try very hard to replicate it. At nine o'clock, the male teacher announces that we will be taught mangal maitreyi. I wonder if it will be as painful as vipassanā. The teacher tells us to relax our bodies, but we, like highly disciplined children, remain sitting cross-legged.

Guruji's voice announces that the objective of this meditation is to transmit the positive vibrations that we have gained from our meditation of the last few days to our loved ones as well as those who may have hurt or harmed us, intentionally or otherwise. In a soft and slow drawl, he talks about loving all beings and also about forgiving oneself and others.

As he speaks, I feel vibrations drifting outward from my body and a gentle coolness fills my chest. Apart from a niggling little loop of pain in my forehead, there is no pain anywhere else. It is a befitting end to the course to further ennoble oneself by not keeping one's purity and love within, but sharing it with the universe.

The mettā meditation ends at ten. I am shivering because of the coolness inside. The experience has been beatific. And now we are free to communicate like normal people. The thought is overwhelming; even more so because I do not want to. I am afraid. I have been safe in my silence and solitude.

As soon as we step out of the hall, there are excited giggles and loud conversation. I recoil in horror at the raucousness. We have been warned to maintain silence around the hall, but all restraint has vanished. The women are beaming and exchanging news and views. I find myself next to the Italian. She is as silent as I am. I am happy and relieved to see that she is not overly keen to converse.

There is no agenda for now; we are free until lunch time and the only thing to do is to head towards the office to retrieve our things. I manage to croak softly to her, 'Shall we?' while gesticulating in the general direction in which everybody is heading. She nods her head and we walk together in companionable silence down the path. I sense that both of us want to savour this moment. As I walk, I wonder what lies ahead and whether I will be able to deal with it.

We reach the office block near the main gate. It is only about a hundred metres from the meditation hall; yet it has seemed like miles away all these days. There is a crowd of people milling about. I recognize some of the staff and some of the male meditators. The Italian and I hang around, unsure of what to do. Once again, I have the feeling I have been locked away for years and have suddenly been thrown into a world I no longer know how to deal with.

Realizing that no one is going to come to our rescue, I meekly make my way to the desk in front of the office and patiently wait for my turn to ask where our phones can be collected from. No one rewards me for my patience and I realize I will have to be bolder. I step forward and ask an ashram staffer where we have to go in a voice which I do not recognize as my own. He gesticulates towards the opposite table. The Italian and I walk up to it to reclaim our belongings.

Now we head back on the path. Instinctively, we feel safer there, instead of with the crowd. I do not attempt to retrieve my phone from the bag. Instead, I start speaking with the Italian. The conversation is slow but meaningful. I am glad to have her and not anyone else as my companion. I ask her if the course has been impactful for her. She answers in the affirmative, but does not sound convincing.

As for me, I cannot really put into words what I have experienced; whether it is the 'white light', the explorations inside the body, the adhishtan sittings or the immense feeling of strength and peace and acceptance. The Italian tells me that she has been unable to sit unmoving for an hour. She also says that the girl in flared pants, has been unable to feel any sensations at all in the entire course! I am puzzled as to how she knows this and cannot believe that one could go through an entire course and not feel one single sensation. I tell her that I have experienced even the cascade effect. She looks totally awed and astonished.

Many women are coming down the path. A group of them stops us and starts praising me for my valiant effort and perseverance. I am astounded and I do not know what to make of it, because I know how much I have faltered along the way. How many times have I envied others their straight-backed and unmoving postures! I also had no idea I was being observed. Not knowing how to receive their compliments, I just smile weakly. The Italian tells me I have been an inspiration for her and many others. I am truly astonished. I have myself been inspired by her so many times: the quiet demeanour, composure and determination.

I am truly humbled at the unexpected praise. I know I have pushed myself beyond my capacity a hundred times and followed rules more faithfully than others, but I have also obsessed and cried and broken down and emerged from the pagoda without lasting even twenty minutes and wandered about, looking at peacocks. I wonder how it has all ended so beautifully.

The Italian and I head towards the dining hall. It is nearly lunch time. It is strange to be walking about at an hour when we would normally be meditating. I savour the sense of freedom.

The American, is in the dining hall with P. We smile broadly at each other and I enquire after P. She still looks weak. My voice is stronger now, though my speech is slow and soft. The American is in great spirits, beaming at everyone. We all bunch together; the same group who met up at the gate a fateful ten days ago, not knowing what was in store for us.

Vipassanā has stripped us of all pretences and we chat like little children. P is the most subdued and I guess she is naturally shy and reticent. After being told that the girl in flared pants did not experience anything at all and seeing the Italian's reaction at mine, I am careful not to talk about my experiences. I realize it may be very disillusioning for others.

The American is holding centre stage and describing some yoga *asanas* or postures. It is creditable that she is so comfortable amongst us. I smile at her excited speech and mannerisms.

All meditators greet each other warmly. We have all undergone the same trials and tribulations and it has bonded us. Age and status, colour or creed; it does not seem to matter. The young sevika is very happy today: finally she can give free rein to her voice and she chats happily with everyone.

The plump Punjabi girl joins us. I learn that this is her eighth course and my mouth falls open in amazement. Suddenly, I realize why she was able to sit so peacefully and still in the meditation hall and why she also always looked unperturbed. She is enjoying the attention that she is getting. The rest of us in the group are all novices. She explains several things to the impressed audience and I listen too, but am more wrapped up in my own thoughts. Also, now that my book again seems like a strong possibility, I am keenly observing and trying to memorize the details of this last day.

It is now almost noon. Apparently, we are free till half past two, when we will once again have to go to the meditation hall for adhishtan. I have never felt so carefree and unoccupied in my life: almost two and a half hours to go and nothing at all to do. I decide this a good time to call my family and my friend.

I am aware that my voice sounds different as I speak to my husband. My speech is slow and deliberate. He asks me to share everything that has happened, but I only want to know if my children are well. Everything else seems unimportant and meaningless. I also know he will not be able to comprehend all that I have experienced here.

I now call the friend who has been responsible for setting me upon the path of Dhamma. He answers the phone right away and without waiting for me to say anything, tells me with a soft laugh that I can thank him. I am silent for a couple of seconds; he has sent me on a journey which has been tremendous in every way and given me a core of steel and mere thanks does not seem to be enough. He asks me if anything in life will ever seem difficult after what I have gone through? At that moment, standing under the shade of a tree in the hot August afternoon, I realize nothing will.

We speak for a long time, sharing experiences, till I realize it is almost one o'clock. I am sleepy. I tell him I will call him later and we say goodbye.

There is no one about. I feel weary and drained. After having climbed the crest, there is nothing more to gain and I hope that I really am strong enough to weather whatever storms life will bring. The feeling of nostalgia and wistfulness is huge. I will never have this kind of refuge and peace again.

An hour of sleep in the afternoon is a luxury I have not known for many days and I exult in it. I stretch out on my bed and close my eyes. After a few minutes of floating and flowing with sensations, I fall asleep.

True to form, I wake up fifteen minutes before the start of the adhishtan session. I wear my hair band once again and reapply the kohl. I am aware that trivial things such as these will have very little meaning once I am back in my world. It is only here that they have taken on the joy and poignancy that they have. I feel more beautiful than I have in years.

The hip pain comes back in full measure in the hall, but I ignore it and it lessens and becomes constant. My thoughts go back in time. So much of the pain and regret and worry seem unnecessary now, but I still can't help thinking of the future. I do know one thing, though; I may or not be able to control what happens, but I can control how I react. Whether I let vicissitudes affect me or not is in my hands. The pain and problems don't go away with meditation or with retreats. How we deal with them, however, can change.

The hour is soon up. It is followed by a short break and then we sit down once again for mettā meditation. I sit with my legs to a side. I am still in pain and I wonder if I am fit to be sending out mettā in this condition. Guruji has said we must not have any solidified sensations in the body during mettā meditation, but my intentions are noble and my heart is full of goodwill and love. Unlike in the mettā session earlier, I do not feel any coolness in my chest, but I do feel faint vibrations moving outwards from my body. Guruji speaks about love and compassion and forgiveness and all beings finding peace. While he does, I realize once again the futility of hate and regret and bitterness.

At quarter to four, we are free to go out of the meditation hall. Once again, it is a strange feeling to be walking about at this time, without any craving for recess and deliverance. I find myself once again with the Italian, the American, P and the girl in flared pants. We stand on the shady walkway and discuss our lives and experiences. The American is from New Orleans and has travelled half the world alone. She is only twenty-eight. P and the girl in flared pants are in their early twenties. The girl in flared pants is extremely cheerful despite the fact that she has not gained much from the course. P is still quiet, though less reticent than before.

The American tells us she wants to get a tattoo to commemorate this vipassanā course. She says she wanted the word 'anicca' on her arm, but realized it would be ironic. She then settled for the word *samta,* which means equanimity, and I think it is a great idea. She wants it in Devnagri, the Hindi script, and asks if I will write it down for her. As it so happens, we both forget.

It would be wonderful to get a tattoo to commemorate and remember this awesome experience. I mull that the *Dhamma chakra* would be an apt symbol of my spiritual journey. I will never forget the sight of the window with spokes in the meditation cell in the pagoda, where I struggled with my body and my mind.

After the girls depart, I sit down on the parapet near the underground toilets where it is cool and dial my friend's number. I have not shared all my experiences with him and he is the only one who can understand, since he is an experienced vipassanā meditator. I lose track of time and soon it is five o'clock.

I head towards the dining hall. I do not mind being silent for a while now. However, in the dining hall, the American and P are sitting together and they call out to me. P, uncharacteristically, initiates the conversation. She asks me if I found what I was looking for. I do not want to share my personal life, but I answer in a firm 'yes'. She asks me what it was. Though I detect no frivolous curiosity in her, I fend off her query with an enigmatic smile and ask if both of them found what they were looking for. The American answers first. She says she had been having a spate of bad luck lately. I do not quite see how vipassanā can help mitigate bad luck, but I listen politely.

P hesitatingly tells me she has been very scared of an important exam that she has to take the following year. I almost balk: after all, one would expect a more meaningful goal or outcome than overcoming fear of an exam and I look at her incredulously. I cannot help asking if such a trivial thing had been bothering her to the extent of coming for such a rigorous course. She answers that it is a very important law exam and she has been getting nightmares about it. Too much money and hard work has been invested and she cannot afford to fail. She says, however, that vipassanā has done nothing for her; she still feels the same palpable fear.

She is almost close to tears and sensing the genuine and deep-rooted fear in her, I tell her I am sure that vipassanā will 'kick in' to rescue her. P is not consoled and I hope that she will find a way out of her problem.

We are joined by the Italian, the girl in flared pants and a few others, including the Punjabi girl. I shyly share that I am planning a book about my experiences here. There are looks of admiration and several 'oohs' and 'aahs'. I ask them with a smile if I can mention all of them in my book, they laugh and readily agree. The Punjabi girl advises me that I should undergo at least one more course before I write my book and I try to explain unsuccessfully to her that my book is about this first experience.

Someone asks the American to show us her tattoo and she obligingly pirouettes around and lifts up her foot and explains the symbolism behind it. What I thought were bleak, bare branches of a tree are actually roots. The tattoo goes further up on her leg and reveals an ear of corn. She explains that her tattoo is symbolic of her ancestry of farming folk.

It is my turn to be asked about the tattoo on my ankle and I show them the leopard with the snake. I tell them I also have another on my back and they ask to see it. Unselfconsciously and in an un-meditator like fashion, I turn around and strip off the shoulder of my tee in full view of everyone and they all laugh and admire the tattoo.

We are back in the hall at six. This is my last evening here. Dusk will be very different when I go back and I will always be thinking of the quiet and peaceful ashram and my peacocks at this hour. This time will never come back; it will be as impermanent as all else.

As we head out to the mini hall for the discourse, I feel a huge lump in my heart. I stop to stare at the Aravalis for several minutes, uncaring of what others might say or feel. Thankfully, they do not interrupt my reverie.

I sit next to the American with my back to the wall. She tells me that she has had the strongest sensations in her legs and she has been able to examine them in one sweeping motion. She does not describe any other sensation or experience and I keep quiet about mine.

Farewells have never been easy for me. The screen announces the last day of vipassanā. It was a cherished day, eagerly awaited, but now that it is here, there is just sadness. Guruji's face comes on. His eyes are closed. When he opens them, he announces that the tenth day is over; a statement that tugs at my heartstrings. Apparently all of us do not share the same view and I hear some laughter from Guruji's television audience. I grimace.

Today's discourse is mostly about Guruji's personal journey on the path of Dhamma. There is no more talk about the technique. After he finishes the discourse, Guruji closes his eyes once again. I feel tears pricking my eyes; then steel myself remembering Guruji's words of wisdom about the futility of attachments. He has shown the way: it is up to me to walk on it. Still, I feel very raw and unmoored as we head back towards the meditation hall.

Tonight, there is no meditation after the discourse. I am glad. Even though the course has impacted me greatly, I am enjoying the sense of freedom after so many days. I also want to speak to my friend again. The others head towards their blocks in groups, but I sit down on the parapet close to the assistant teacher's house and dial his number. During the course, it would have been unthinkable to do so at this hour.

He and I talk for a long time. Finally, I see the girl in flared pants approaching me from the triangular walkway in the semi-darkness. I gesticulate for her to wait. She halts abruptly and seeing that I am occupied, turns around and walks away. The Italian also appears after a while and looks astonished to see me still on the phone. She also walks away. I am perhaps the only one who is having a phone conversation at this hour in the darkness.

After a while, my body starts to ache and I start to walk about. I am surprised to feel strong currents running down my legs as I walk. It is very late now. I end the conversation and head back towards my room. My block is too quiet and suddenly I am afraid of being alone. Where is everyone? I walk to the block next to mine. The girl in flared pants, the Italian and the American all stay in this block. There is not much activity in their block either. I do not know their rooms.

Suddenly, I hear laughter and voices coming from one of the rooms. Instinctively, I know my soul sisters are in there. I walk towards the room and tap on the window. Immediately, there are startled and horrified cries from inside. The door is gingerly opened. The American, the girl in flared pants, the Italian and another girl I do not know very well are in the room. They are breathless with fear and I smile in amazement. How can one be afraid after having dealt with all kinds of demons here? When I walk in, I see that there are tarot cards spread out on the bed. I shake my head in disbelief. That is not all. There are pens and paper lying about the room and the girls are busy writing down each others' e-mails and phone numbers. I had agonized over the theft of a pen and paper, while others already had tarot cards, writing material and even phones in their possession!

My friend has told me that it is not advisable to be in each others' rooms at the end of the course. This is because there would be defilements in each meditator's room. We have already been told not to shake hands or embrace, but I suspect that rule has already been broken by most and of course, the girls are huddled together in the room right now. They excitedly ask for my phone number and e-mail and I ask them for theirs. I ask where P is and they nonchalantly tell me she retired to her room a long time back. I realize P is truly haunted by her demons and feel very sorry that the course has not exorcised them.

I leave the girls to their revelry after promises to keep in touch. Tomorrow morning is going to be hurried. We have been told we will be free to leave after breakfast and I suspect everyone will be in a rush to leave. I walk slowly towards my room. Now that the course is over, there is no urgency to sleep or rest, but it is late and I am feeling drained and tired.

The night is cool. I open the curtain of my little window and look out into the courtyard at the lamp post which was the beacon for thousands of dreaded grasshoppers. I have learnt to accept so much adversity here and deal with horror, revulsion and pain. I think once again about the future, but it is not mine to choose and I give up trying to find answers and solutions. Que sera sera. I will deal with stuff when it happens. I am clear as to what must *not be*; the rest I shall see about.

I fall off to sleep at around one, with tears of gratitude in my eyes.

12

THE END OF THE JOURNEY

THE DAY AWAKENS LIKE ANY OTHER. THE SAME DARKNESS, the same sounds of wakefulness and the bell ringing near the meditation hall. But there is a different feel to the day. In two hours, we will no longer be confined to the little boundary of the ashram.

We are still required to meditate for two hours till half past six. Anxiousness about the time and thoughts of going home make me agitated and results in considerable pain. I am glad when Guruji announces anicca. Strangely, it is only five.

The male teacher says there will now be a discourse and that the English discourse students should go to the mini hall. I had not expected a discourse today. It is not yet dawn. I no longer walk slowly, lost in contemplation. Though we all head together to the mini hall, none of us talk much. The silhouette of the Aravalis is a beautiful indigo, but I do not stand and stare. It seems to have lost some of their charisma and evocativeness. Such is human nature, I tell myself. We pine for what we cannot have and cannot appreciate what we do.

I sit erect on the cushion right in front in the mini hall. Guruji appears, but does not speak. Instead, he starts reciting the dohas that are sung from six to half past six every day. His eyes are closed. I watch for a while; then my eyes close too and I involuntarily start meditating.

The pain rises in my hips and legs and knees; then it starts swelling in my back like in the first few days of the course. I have not been able to sit in adhishtan for a while now, but now I am like a block of stone. I observe the tremendous pain as Guruji's chanting continues. Sadness, like the pain, rises and threatens to overwhelm me, but I do not let it sway my resolve. I lose track of time. I only open my eyes when the singing stops and Guruji starts speaking. I can see the dawn from the windows of the mini hall. I remain sitting.

Guruji says that when we generate a vibration of craving or aversion out of ignorance, this vibration starts getting attuned with the negative vibrations in the universe. This way, our cravings and aversions get stronger. However, the same rule applies to positive vibrations. When we generate vibrations of anti-craving or anti-aversion, we get tuned in to positive vibrations and Dhamma starts helping us.

Human life is very valuable, Guruji says, because only humans have the faculty and the ability to purify their minds and be liberated. He exhorts us to open the gateway of the *Brahmnic* plane and the *Nibbanic* peace within. Then he smiles and says that though he has been deriding most old traditions in our country, there is one old tradition that he likes very much. This is the tradition of *Gurudakshina*, in which a pupil gives an offering to his teacher for imparting his knowledge to him. 'After all,' he says jocularly, 'I was born in a business family and I must serve my self-interest. There should be a fat fee for the fat teacher.' I wonder what this selfless and philanthropic man could want. But Guruji only wants that whenever we meditate at home, we should practise mettā meditation and wish for all beings to share in our merits. This way, our vibrations of loving kindness would reach him too and this would be his remuneration. If we do not do this, he warns smilingly, the technique will not work for us. I marvel at the benevolence of our great teacher.

Guruji now asks us to practise mettā meditation. I close my eyes again. Guruji starts speaking in a very low and soft voice; the softest in all these days. He asks for the merits we have acquired in these ten days to be shared with all beings. He asks for our peace and harmony to be shared as well. 'May all beings be happy,' he says. 'May all beings be peaceful. May all beings be liberated.'

There is silence. I open my eyes. Guruji's eyes are closed and he is sitting in deep concentration. I turn around slightly to look at the clock and am amazed to see it is a quarter past six. Once again, I have sat unmoving and still for an hour and fifteen minutes.

The television set is switched off. Guruji is gone.

We head slowly up the path, wondering what to do next. Just then, the young sevika appears in the grassy patch to the left and frantically ushers us towards the main meditation hall. Surprised, we hasten towards it. The meditators in the main hall are all sitting with eyes closed. The screen is on and Guruji is chanting. We take our places and close our eyes. The mettā meditation is not over yet. The chanting stops after a while and Guruji is silent. I try and send out the same vibrations that emanated from me yesterday, but right now, they are too feeble. However, I have the same lightness of being and tremendous feeling of goodwill and forgiveness towards one and all.

After a few minutes, Guruji sings the lines that I remember from many mornings in the dining hall, while I battled acute loneliness. Then, once again, he starts speaking. He recites the words which I will henceforth verbalize in my mind each time I sit down for mettā meditation: 'I pardon all those who have hurt me or harmed me, intentionally or unintentionally, by their deeds of body, speech or mind. I seek pardon from all those who I might have hurt or harmed, knowingly or unknowingly. All are my friends. None is my enemy. May all share my merits, my peace, my harmony, my Dhamma. May all be happy. May all be peaceful. May all be liberated.'

With this, the course truly does come to an end. Guruji starts singing once again. Guruji's wife comes into view. Guruji takes off his collar mic and they both stand up. With their hands raised in benediction, they move slowly out of the room together, still singing the dohas.

We all rise. Following the actions of the others, I start taking the covers off my cushions. We take them to the bottom of the hall and place them in a heap. The cushions are also lifted up and stacked against a wall. This done, we are free to leave. I want to thank the teachers for their guidance and mentoring, but they have not waited for praise or gratitude and have left. They must already be preparing to leave for their own homes.

I am like a ship, which has been left unmoored on the high seas. I am a ship which is new to the ocean, but I am a ship which is sturdy and which must reach the other shore.

My last memories of that day are of taking pictures of the pristine white pagoda in the glorious and warm sunshine of that morning, as I stand alone on the walkway, which has been the place where I have experienced heartbreaking loneliness, sadness and regret; a place where I have agonized and ached and marveled as I gazed at my shrine.

There is a peacock atop the pagoda and I am glad I have been able to capture it in my camera as well. It has symbolized and meant a lot during my stay here and given me my cherished talisman.

I had found my liberation, and the journey which started with pain, apprehension and ignorance was over.

EPILOGUE

❧❦❧

$\mathcal{I}$N THE SUMMER OF THE FOLLOWING YEAR, I DID something which I had vowed I would not: I went back to the ashram for a second time. I went ostensibly to renew my strength and wisdom, but in reality, it had been a very trying and testing year and I remembered my sanctuary. All the strength and knowledge of the first time had faded over the months, though the tremendous changes I had undergone did help me through many crises.

Like a wounded bird seeking refuge to heal, I headed back in the blazing month of May. My heart filled with gladness at seeing the ashram again. I never thought I would come back to this site of overwhelming emotion, endurance and pain. The loneliness was frightening; I met no soul sisters, whose silent companionship I could rely on for courage during the course.

The course turned out to be very different from what I had expected. Firstly, I thought adhishtan would be easy for me. It was not; and I went through the same agonies of pain and resilience to reach the stage where I could sit with a fair amount of equanimity. Perhaps the months prior had eroded all of it. I think there was much more equanimity the first time over, when I really did not know what to expect. This time around, I knew no miracles would happen and none did. No 'white lights' and no cascades. Vipassanā guarantees one no miracles.

I took notes during the second course and didn't feel guilty about writing down my most poignant thoughts. If I don't share these here, this book would be incomplete because a piece of my heart would be left unshared: On Day

Zero, I folded my hands in my room and told God that I was leaving my world behind, with all its pains, sorrows and regrets and I asked God to look after it. Isolation breeds many unreasonable fears. I also asked God to keep me from pain. Then I realized I was here for the purpose of accepting both pain and joy equally in my life. My hopes fled in that instant and I was left feeling more alone than ever. Though I had my God with me, He would be nothing but a silent spectator and I could not call upon Him for succour.

On the first day itself, I realized once again that we always crave for things to happen in a particular fashion. When they don't, there's always sorrow or pain. I heard the powerful words '*Anattā gan me, anattā tan me*' on the first day and shivers ran down my spine. I had thought of these words often in the months since the last course and missed the strength of their vibration.

We started the course as usual with observation of breath. On the notice board, I read the words which must have been there during the first day of the first course as well, but I had not seen them:

'Observing breath after breath, the mind becomes still.

Unwavering, it finds peace and finally finds its liberation.'

I would think of these words countless times in the first three days and noticed the change in my mind and mental processes as I attempted to do exactly this.

I observed my beloved peacocks and life around closely this time around and I realized animals live in accordance with the laws of nature, quite unlike us evolved beings. I longed for a life as simple as theirs – clean and uncomplicated. I wanted to live by the passage of the sun and the stars. Out there in the ashram, we really did live like creatures in the wild and that was part of our healing and evolving process. It was a good, clean and wholesome lifestyle, just as Nature intended: waking with the birds and animals, resting when the day is at its hottest and sleeping with the awakening of the stars. Along with all this was a deep sense of dignity of the body and mind – a dignity we let get blemished with our unhealthy lifestyles, full of vices.

As an old student, I was allowed to go into the pagoda from the second day itself and I did. I went in to my cell in pitch dark at half past four in the morning. My heart was pounding and it took nerves of steel to close the door of the cell and be swallowed by the darkness of the confines within: a door which did not lock. I only became aware of the possible hazards of this when one of the sevikas admonished me not to go into the pagoda at half past four, as it was not safe to do so. I had to take special permission from the female teacher to meditate in the pagoda at such an early hour.

I remained the only woman to repeatedly go into the pagoda to meditate at that hour. Often, I would hear a hacking sound or a footstep in the darkness. They were all from the men's side of the pagoda and they would frighten me. I would imagine a man barging into my cell. I felt scared, weak, vulnerable and helpless, yet I carried on meditating in the cell in the darkness.

On the third night, there was a terrible storm and the electricity went off. It was almost impossible to sleep in the oven-like atmosphere of the closed room, but I did eventually fall off to sleep, bathed in my own sweat and trying to fight my demons. Most of the time, there would be no electricity in that terrible month of May and we would spend hours meditating in the hall without even the draught of fans and rest in our rooms with the stifling air threatening to suffocate us. Most of us meditators took to splashing buckets of water on the floor of our rooms to cool the room down and many slept with their doors open. I slid around on my hands and knees often in the water I had splashed upon the floor of the room to cool it down. It must have made for a strange sight indeed.

On the fourth morning, there was complete calm, as if the

storm had never happened. A day washed anew, after a night of such turbulence. I imagined the years of storms within and how much havoc they must have wreaked inside, with no hope or chance of rebuilding or rejuvenating what had been eroded. As Nature does in the universe, so it does within.

I was hungry the first few days because we could not eat after eleven in the morning and I willed myself not to look at the new meditators eating and having tea at five in the evening. I stole fruit yet again, but did not eat it and I returned it furtively to the dining hall just before it got rotten. Even a simple wrongdoing like stealing a fruit caused so much strain in my mind. It would haunt me while I meditated and it occurred to me that there must be a tremendous level of strain inside for all the wrongdoings of thirty-eight years.

On the fourth night, my head became so heavy, I felt it would burst. I did not know it just then, but the surgical operation of the mind was underway in a big way and the pain would get worse with every passing day.

The only solace was the beauty of the ashram and of its flora and fauna and the care which was taken to look after us meditators. The water in the coolers was too cold, so earthen pots had been placed alongside the coolers so that the meditators could mix the water and make it less cold. I came down with a throat infection because I drank the really cold water for the first couple of days; the heat was just too intense, but I had forgotten how fragile and sensitive my body was.

Things had improved at the ashram. The bed linen was washed and pressed and laid upon my cot when I arrived and I did not need to use my own linen, which I had carried with me. I had come prepared this time. I had carried my own bucket, toilet-cleaning equipment, my own linen and my own comforter, which, of course, I had absolutely no need of in that terribly hot month of May.

The food was good, as always. There were delicious mangoes placed in oversized utensils of ice-cold water and always plenty of yogurt and fresh salads. The grassy, overgrown patch on the side of the path next to the teacher's quarters – where, last year, the snake had been thrown – had been manicured and landscaped. It was a beautiful sloping garden, where, from the fifth day onwards, meditators would just lie in the breaks between meditation sessions. They would sprawl out flat upon the grass. I was too inhibited to do so at first, but I did so eventually and the cool grass upon my back and the sight of the laburnums and gulmohurs outlined against the sky was succour to my mind. It was a mind which was being invaded with sharp, cruel steel and I struggled constantly with the pain.

A bush of jasmine had been planted near the water cooler next to the meditation hall and the smell of its sweet perfume wafted around at night. The management and workers of the ashram had placed pots of water around the ashram for thirsty birds and animals and there was a tap of water always running slowly in the grove where the peacocks lived. They would all mostly congregate there. It was far too hot for even these creatures to move; even when we passed very close to them. I wondered how we could meditate those four hours in the blazing heat of the afternoon every day.

On the sixth day, I read the thought for the day, which I had forgotten from the previous time and which had inspired and awed me even then:

> *Strive ardently O man and burn*
> *Purity comes from burning away the dross*
> *Gold must pass through a crucible in order to be refined.*

I was awestruck once again at the import of these words. I was burning. I was burning in the heat of the worst month of summer. I was also burning within my mind as I struggled with the pain of the operation. And my body burnt each time I sat down in the meditation hall. The feeling that I was on fire and that flames were lapping at my body would be there hour after hour in the hall.

The laburnum and gulmohur trees were in full bloom in the sizzling heat and they were heartbreakingly lovely. I chose perhaps the most difficult month in which to go and meditate. A fearsome *loo* would blow in through the open door of the meditation hall. My head would often reel. The last meal for old students was at eleven in the morning and I survived that ordeal for eight days, but eventually fell sick with the heat and lack of food. I was always counting time and days. Unlike last time, there were no expectations and I was dismayed to learn that I could not feel any of the wonderful sensations of last time. I rallied quickly after disappointment each time, however, being acutely aware of the fact that this technique was not about how much one could achieve, but how much equanimity one could maintain in the face of adversity.

What I learnt from the second course is that there is never any end to craving. When there was humongous pain in my pelvis and my back, I would wish for at least one to go away. When the back pain cooled, I would remain agitated, waiting for the pelvic pain to subside. By and by, the pelvic pain would ease, but I would keep wishing for it to disappear. Even when the whole body was free of pain, there would be agitation about the duration of the meditation period and the mind would constantly be stuck on the clock. I would want to be outdoors, even when there was really nothing to do outdoors and the sole reason all of us would keep coming back to the meditation hall hour after hour and day after day was because there was nothing else to do.

There is no end to craving and so there is no end to suffering.

I came to the second course not for miracles, but for wisdom. Many forms of the same answers came to me, one after another; twisted, convoluted, clear and cloudy; but all of the same essence. I did not lose my link with reality. My voice remained clear and audible as I spoke to the teacher. I also looked at other meditators. I did not spend my time in the room ruminating. I was already undergoing too deep an introspection while meditating. I would fall off to sleep every opportunity I got. I wanted to forget. I wanted to shun the demons that danced within my head.

No miracles or magic happened. I trudged through the entire course like a beginner. But something important was transpiring within. I happened to ask the female teacher, a different one this time, early on during the course if it was alright to have 'background' thought while feeling sensations. She told me that in fact, it was desired, as it was the only way the subconscious could throw up buried or suppressed emotions. So, for the first time, I let myself feel my pain while meditating. As I allowed my mind to touch upon forbidden subjects and let the dance of memories play out in my mind, I felt the surgical operation of the brain that Guruji would talk about. During the first course, I had not let my thoughts wander to painful thoughts during meditation, but this time around, my mind had a free rein to feel all the anguish that still lay somewhere deep within.

The 'surgical operation' was indeed painful. So painful that I would start heaving and sobbing with soundless, racking sobs, which would subside as abruptly as they began. My mind was split open with pain as I meditated in forty-five degrees heat day after day, hour after hour. One afternoon, it threw up such painful memories that I knew I was going to break down in a big way in the meditation hall. In the midst of the session, I ran away from the hall and looked for a place to hide and cry. I found the niche near the dormitory on one side of the triangular walkway and hid myself there. I cried as I have never cried before. The buried pain was coming out. I could not stop. I knew it would almost be time for the break. Suddenly afraid and ashamed of being found, I walked quickly to my room.

Exhaustion and a piercing anguish overcame me and I fell upon the floor on my knees, next to my cot. I asked God for help. I knew I should not, this course was not about asking God or any higher power to intervene; that would defeat the purpose of it all, but I could not help it. I had flouted the rules by carrying my holy book with me and I felt no shame in taking it out and running my hand over it then in supplication. Perhaps God listened, perhaps He did not. I could continue with my meditation, but the anguish never receded. My intrinsic determination forced me to face pain like I had never done before. I looked it squarely in the eye and saw my life clearly for what it was and what it was going to be. It was all about choices.

As the painful thoughts and memories coursed through my willing mind and I struggled for equanimity, the law of nature worked slowly for me. Even as I remained unaware of the change, those brief moments of equanimity coalesced and slowly started eradicating the pain from my mind. Clarity started replacing the anguish, as the days went by slowly and painfully. Each time this would happen, my body would convulse and I would cry those silent, racking sobs. That is when I would know that some sankhāra buried within, had left me. They left much wisdom in their wake.

By the seventh day, my body was twitching and jerking as if on fire when I sat down to meditate. I thought of the analogy of the crucible constantly and remembered Guruji's words in a discourse where he said we had come here to burn. I was burning, literally and metaphorically.

By the eighth day, my spirit was flailing badly. My throat infection had spread to my chest. I could 'feel' it with my razor sharp insight regarding sensations. My mind would penetrate easily inside my chest and I could 'see' the spread of infection. I was very ill. Of course, the thought of giving up never occurred to me. That would have been unacceptable to my proud, determined spirit and an affront to my own ego, but, most of all, I needed to be cleansed completely. Feverish and weak, I kept going back to the meditation hall.

The eighth day was as monumental as the one last time. Tired of feeling like a failure, I did my little SWOT analysis of the situation this time around as well. The only difference was that I had my little notepad and pen with me. I felt no qualms in carrying it with me this time: I was an old meditator and if I could think thoughts; well, I could write them down. So I did my analysis of the pros and cons of the situation and once again took comfort from what I had gained than what I had not.

When I woke up on the ninth day, I reeled in the room and nearly fell. I grabbed on to the wall for support. I was very weak and sick. I was also nauseous, probably because of a mild heatstroke. I almost crawled back into my bed, but sheer will and fear of a feeling of self-defeat made me get dressed and walk out of my room. I headed, contrary to even my expectations; into the pagoda. Battling nausea, weakness and a fever, I meditated unmoving in the complete darkness. It was a huge feat of strength, determination and courage.

The pain was intense. I do not know how I managed to get through that day. I remember I just wanted the course to get over and for me to leave. I had battled my demons for enough days to know that most of them could cause me no more pain.

After the morning session and breakfast, my spirit was truly broken. I sat on the side of the triangular walkway after breakfast, with my body turned away from the path, towards the grove where the peacocks lived and I cried softly, with the tears falling on to the hard, parched earth of the empty grove. A girl who sat right in front in the meditation hall and whom I kept emulating for her unwavering stance, was walking as usual on the walkway; much as I had done during the first course.

I was ashamed and embarrassed, but there was only one more day to go: the day which did not really count and I would never see her again, even though her life, too, had been intertwined with mine in some strange manner, like N's had been. The morning was heartbreakingly beautiful, with just a tiny hint of coolness before the day would start blazing in all its fury and I only had tomorrow to go through before I could leave. But I had no real hope that life outside would be easier. There were too many choices to be made in the outside world.

Even as I cried with my face turned away from the world, I knew I had let go of many of the karmic imprints stored in my psyche, in the last few days. The conditioning of our minds is the biggest hurdle to leading a life of peace.

I did not give up my endeavours. On the morning of the last day, I forced myself to go into the pagoda for the last time. Shivering with fever and incredibly weak, I meditated with a concentration that would have put Vishvamitra to shame. Vishvamitra was a Hindu sage who practiced severe penance to such an extent that even Indra, the God of the heavens, was shaken and sent down an *apsara* or nymph, to seduce Vishvamitra and break his penance. I concentrated so hard that a pure ring of energy formed around my body and began to travel slowly down. It was strong and true and unbroken and it overrode the terrible pain.

The ring moved up and down, slowly, powerfully. When I could not hold on anymore, perhaps because my mind was subconsciously keeping a track of the time, I opened my eyes and shifted my body a little. Then I slowly got up and moved out of the cell and into the open. It was nearly half past five and the world was resplendent. I loved being outdoors at this time of the morning, when

I had completed my own voluntary hour of adhishtan. Meditating alone in the pagoda always gave me a sense of freedom. I could emerge from the cell without feeling guilty and enjoy the early morning while others meditated in the hall. And though I always went back in after a short break, I could never really put in another consolidated effort to meditate.

On the last day, I could feel no currents running down my legs. I felt pretty much like a failure as far as the technique was concerned, but I was aware that I had gained a lot of wisdom and shed a lot of ignorance. The last course had been amazing and tremendous. I had felt victorious as if I had scaled insurmountable peaks. What I could do with my body had taken precedence over everything else. The painful realization of being fallible came with this course but it also brought about a kind of wisdom that I never obtained the last time: a very deep wisdom, even with the sense of defeat and fallibility. I had no visions of being tathāgata. All visions of glory had gone and they had left a helpless, tormented person in their wake, but a person who did not shy away from pain: someone who stood under the blazing skies and let the screaming pain of mental agony flow in torrents through her mind. An agony that was far worse than the bodily agony that I had experienced the last time.

The last day was forlorn and somnolent. I hardly spent any time with any co-meditators after the vow of silence was lifted. I was ill and preferred to sleep most of the day. It was too hot to be outdoors like the last time, anyway. My voice on the phone when I finally retrieved my phone from the office was steady and clear, unlike the slow drawl of the last time. I did not talk for long. My friend was surprised at my brevity and the hardness in my voice.

As I walked towards the office block on the tenth day to retrieve my phone, tears rolled down my face. I was glad I was carrying an umbrella to shield me from the fearsome sun. There was none of the glow and luminosity of the previous time. It was the wisdom which was making me cry.

The last time around, I had felt tathāgata. I had felt liberated. But I had not been truly liberated. This I only learnt when I came back in that terrible month of May. I learnt the truth about myself. The state of being truly tathāgata takes several lifetimes. Ignorance is a great comforter. I was crying because I was not ignorant anymore.

I was grateful for that illusion from the last course. It served me well many times. I wrote this book. But now I knew that I could, at this stage, only strive to be an *ariya* or a noble one. There was a very long path ahead of me. This was the knowledge that would truly help me in my life. There was no more illusion.

I left the ashram as usual with a lump in my heart. It had been my sanctuary and teacher twice already.

***

This book could have ended on a note of victory and the sweet taste of feeling tathāgata, but it would not have been true. As I end this soliloquy, I am aware that life is not so much about achievement as it is about wisdom. I am not liberated, but maybe I am on the path to eventual liberation. I acknowledge my own fallibility, vulnerability and mortality. Acceptance and equanimity can lead to tremendous changes in one's life. When we stop struggling against the odds that life throws before us and just observe them for what they are, they sometimes throw up the unexpected. Too much of our life is struggle to make things go according to our will. Too much of our lives is pain for what does not go according to plan. When we accept with equanimity, the law of nature starts working for us and we align with the grandeur of the universe.